Early R

Fred Falkner
5.0 out of 5 stars
An educational and throughly entertaining account of a bleak time

"Berkoff's account of the World War II bombing of London from the perspective of a young boy is thoroughly captivating. His very witty and clever style entertains one while learning about those early years of the war filtered through a lad in the unique culture of East London. I particularly enjoyed the organization of the chapters with a prescript setting up the topic, a script detailing experiences and views, and a post script expressing views molded by the passage of time. Well researched and amazing detail."

hg
5.0 out of 5 stars
A fascinating and humorous account of a young boy's London life during WWII.

"Hard to believe that there could be humor in the terrifying horror of the London Blitz. But this author, who, as a young child, survived the ordeal, finds the "lighter side" of that experience. A very personal memoir: well written, informative, and surprisingly funny. I particularly liked the way he structured the different chapters, and was fascinated by his comments on the great Winston Churchill."

Amazon Customer
5.0 out of 5 stars
A treasury of little known facts about life as a child in London during WWII

"Very well written and researched from life experience, this book proved most enjoyable for me as a former Londoner. I liked both the humor and the variety of stories told from the point of view of a young man with the typical East Ender's canny pragmatism, edginess and obvious dislike of anywhere away from the sound of Bow Bells.. His use of the vernacular is delightful and brings back strong memories of the typical London Taxi driver's constant commentary and wit. A very entertaining read."

Dan Taylor
4.0 out of 5 stars
A fun (and educational) read about a heart-wrenching topic

"This was certainly a different look at this topic, and one that provided new insights to this middle-aged Aussie as to what the war in England was really like. I felt Charles's humourous style was a legacy of coping with the ordeals of his childhood, and were good examples of the powerful defense mechanism that was used to overcome the horror of The Blitz. I may of course be totally wrong about this, and Charles may have developed his sense of humour once he emigrated to the US, but I doubt it. I found the views on Dresden and Sir Winston Churchill to be of major interest, because they came from someone who lived through the thick of it - it just left me wanting to hear more such views, hence the four and not five stars."

Kindle Customer
4.0 out of 5 stars
A dark time told in a witty style

"I thoroughly enjoyed Charles Berkoff's new book about his experiences during the London Blitz in World War II. The author has a great sense of humor and his light-hearted account of this critical phase of Britain's war with Nazi Germany – as experienced by a young boy – is highly recommendable."

Robert W. Dahlin
5.0 out of 5 stars
Recollections of a small boy surviving the Blitz

"I completely enjoyed reading the book. It was well written, and was factual as will as humorous in spots. It detailed the experiences of a small boy caught up in the terrible London bombings during world war two. I have read a lot about the war, but never from the first hand experiences of a young boy and his real life reactions to the conflict. I recommend the book to anyone interested in history."

Also by Charles Berkoff

Novel
PreMedicated Murder

Short Story Collection
The Catcher Goes Awry
…and Other Odds & Sods

The Lighter Side of

London's Bloody Blitz

As Seen Through the Eyes of a Young Boy

Charles Berkoff

Dedication

To all those Londoners who survived The Blitz
—and to those who didn't.

And to my dear wife, Heide, for her enthusiastic support,
and her willingness to listen to my wartime stories with
extraordinary patience and fortitude.

Does it ever end?

Acknowledgments

While, in these pages, I focus on the humor that sustained me in my efforts to survive the London Blitz, on a far more serious note I want to record my deep debt of gratitude to those who literally kept me alive during those six long years of World War II—gratitude that has grown steadily over the years. Without their help, I would have no need to acknowledge others who, much later, guided me in my efforts to record my experiences.

First I lived it, then survived it, and only then was I ready to describe it. Eighty years later.

Top of the "thank you" list must be my parents. Whether it was well-conceived strategic thinking, intuitive reasoning, or pure dumb luck, I can only speculate. Nevertheless, because of them, I arrived safely at my twelfth birthday, shaken, hardened perhaps, but basically intact. So thank you, Mum and Dad. You did your job. Your little boy is now a little old man, and he doesn't forget.

On the home front, others were also there to help and protect me. They were the Civil Defence workers of the

Air Raid Precaution, and the National Ambulance and Fire Services. They patrolled the neighborhood, day and night, doing their duty. ARP wardens kept me away from unexploded bombs, hustled me into air-raid shelters when necessary, and prevented me from exploring crashed planes and unsafe buildings. Many lost their lives in the Blitz. Fathers of friends. Mothers too. How can I not admire and be grateful to them?

Beyond the home front, I must bow to those who fought for us further afield: the service men and women, Britons and British Commonwealth, Americans and other Allies. Many died. We lived. And we remember.

One arguably unlikely addition to my list of heroes has to be Winnie. Winston Churchill. He proved to be a force that even a young boy could feel: his strength, his determination, the sound of his speech-impedimented voice. Hard to believe, isn't it, that one man whom I'd never actually met, but come close to meeting, could make such a difference to a kid? But he did. So I salute you, Mr. C., you're one of the few aristocrats I know of who merited that kind of respect.

These, then, were the people to whom I pay tribute. To offer "thanks" is so inadequate. The best we can do is to remember them, and to hope that their sacrifices inspire others.

Now, as I gather and describe those indelibly vivid memories, I turned not to one editor but two: Elizabeth Huntoon Coursen and Dora Hopkins. Thank you both for practicing your art with consummate skill and enthusiasm.

To the staff of CEBRAL Publications, what do I say to them? Great job, people. Pia Perkins, Rosie Purvis, Susan DeMarinis: you're the best!

And the BBC, the British Broadcasting Company. Yes, they too played a role. Their archives, in particular their sound files of World War II, proved to have an unexpected impact. The sounds of Winston Churchill's voice, air raid sirens, Royal Air Force Spitfires in action, airplanes screaming to earth, descending bombs, and the final seconds of a V1 rocket before it crashes stimulated the release of the associated emotions from within me. For better *and* worse, I could relive the thrills and fears, the excitement and the dread of London's Bloody Blitz.

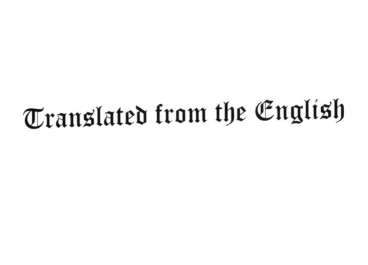

Translated from the English

"War is hell"

William Tecumseh Sherman
US Army General

Yes, but …

Contents

Preface

"The Blitz? Not another bloody book on World War II," my old London pal, Peter, groaned. "There are hundreds of 'em. And surely dozens on the Blitz itself."

Since Peter was a well-published author and editor, I knew I'd be well-advised to listen to him.

"This is…different," I offered, as convincingly as I could.

"Yeah, that's what they all say."

"No, really. This one is a highly personalized account written from the perspective of a young boy who was there. Slap-bang in the middle of it all. I was that boy. I was in London for every damned air raid we endured. I didn't miss a single bomb; fortunately, every single bomb missed me. Great Britain and France declared war on Nazi Germany on September 3, 1939. I was six, almost seven at the time. And nearly thirteen at the end of the war in mid-1945. The memories are all vividly intact."

"What's the book called?"

"That proved to be quite a challenge. I struggled to find an appealing title. Something different. Instinctively, I was drawn to some kind of a play on words. As you know, that's the way I lean. Unfortunately, nothing leaped out at me. It really was a struggle. In fact, my first title was My Struggle. Unfortunately, that translates to Mein Kampf in German, Adolf Hitler's political manifesto. Using that would be like paying homage to the evil bastard. Then there's Alex Comfort and his phenomenally successful The Joy of Sex, I rather liked The Joy of Six. After all, I was a somewhat joyous six-year-old at the start of World War II." I paused. "Okay, in the absence of a joyous response from you, I'll continue. Something Shakespearean, perhaps? He's always good for a title or a quotation. The Comedy of Terrors maybe? Think The Comedy of Errors. That would be appropriate, don't you think?" Another pause. Another absence of a response. "I guess you don't think."

"No. I don't. I hope you have something a bit more creative."

"Since it's all about the Blitz, I thought I should have that word in the title. I toyed with Brit's Blitz for a while, and even though the Germans spread their Blitz around the country, I didn't feel right sharing it with the rest of the UK; my focus is primarily on London. So the struggle continued. And that's when I ran into titler's block: no more titles. Not a one. I then found myself staring at Landy, my dog, and in total frustration, snapped, 'Bloody Blitz!' And that was my 'aha' moment. I'd heard the phrase 'Bloody Blitz!' so many times during the war, I lost count. So, however many it was, I was ready to make it one more.

But I'll elucidate a little, and call it 'London's Bloody Blitz.' And just to be trendy, I'll add an absurdly long description, making it an absurdly long title. To wit: *The Lighter Side of London's Bloody Blitz as Seen Through the Eyes of a Young Boy.* Wajathink?"

"I don't know. Using the word 'bloody' is tricky, isn't it? You'd have to explain its use to most American readers."

"Yes, you're right, of course. I'll have to tell them that in American English, 'bloody' usually means blood-related. In British English, however, in addition to meaning blood-related, 'bloody' is commonly used to express anger, annoyance, or shock. It's also used simply for emphasis. Examples could include: 'Bloody hell!—what was that?' 'It's bloody cold outside.' 'He bloody well deserved it!' In my neck of the London woods, we use the word 'bloody' in its colloquial sense all the time."

Peter persisted, "And what's this 'lighter side' all about?"

"Well, from the perspective of a six-year-old, the Blitz was a totally different experience from my everyday life. Some scary moments too, of course, but above all, it was exciting. Exhilarating. And often funny. So many new adventures. So different from my everyday existence. An unpredictability such that I could no longer expect to sleep in my own bed. One night it was a street shelter, another it was the platform of a tube station, yet another was a Morrison shelter inside the house. It gave new meaning to the phrase "sleeping around." How could it not be the most extraordinary experience in a young boy's life? And I couldn't help notice that, with typical British aplomb, those around me simply 'got on with it.'

Brit Grit at its best.

"Even though I was too young to understand the full impact of war, I could do no less.

"Daytime air raids came first when the London sky was essentially filled with hundreds of German bombers and their fighter escorts. All too few British Hurricanes and Spitfires did their best to intervene. Aerial dogfights. Planes twisting and turning. Pursuing and pursued. Parachutes drifting earthwards. What a sight! Surely this was the ultimate spectacle for a young boy. Better than the movies could ever capture.

"Then came the nighttime raids. From within our street shelter, we could hear the whistle of descending bombs, explosions, and the angry noise of British shellfire. The characteristic sound of a descending enemy plane on its way to a fiery end was always welcome, but only after we had survived its crash.

"Fire trucks and ambulances rushing from one site of urgent need to the next. Bodies being carried away on stretchers. Dead? Alive? Somewhere in between? Grim-faced, grimy-faced firemen, exhausted rescue workers, and Air Raid Precaution Wardens amid the rubble, digging out whatever, whoever was left. These sights I saw. And remember.

"As interminable as an attack always seemed to be, it eventually came to an end. The wail of the 'All Clear' siren announced a welcome period of relief. But for how long? How long before the next inevitable wave of the Luftwaffe's fury? Meanwhile, we'd trudge back home. Sleep-deprived, but intact. At daybreak, like vultures swooping down on carrion, my friends and I would roam the streets competing for the scattered, jagged fragments of shrapnel, many still quite hot. I was very proud of my collection."

Peter continued. "A little tasteless, then, isn't it? Having 'fun' at the expense of your fellow countrymen as they struggled and fought for their lives?"

"No, my story is *never* at their expense. The targets of the fun are the Nazis and the predicaments in which we found ourselves. That's the way we handled the horror."

My conversation with Peter ended in promises: I promised I'd send him a copy of my completed manuscript; he promised he might read it. It was the best deal I could make.

And so, as Peter's voice faded away, I reflected further on that memorable period of my life. My small, limited, prewar world had rapidly expanded with unexpected adventures. Both welcome and not. Gradually, the "lighter side" of it began to diminish. Or at least darken a little. In the latter stages of the war, when I was five or six years older, I began to develop a more realistic awareness of the threat and reality of death. By then, Germany's V-1 flying bombs and V-2 rockets had had their effect. The innocence of my six-year-old self had inexorably yielded to the developing fear of a war-weary twelve-year-old. I was a true "Child of the Blitz." Nevertheless, humor sustained me, sustained us. Humor, and cups of strong British tea. Winston Churchill helped.

But before I get too caught up in my story, I should present a little background. The UK, and later that same day, France, formally went to war with Germany on September 3, 1939. The conflict lasted six years. Soon after the Nazis occupied France in mid-1940, the British Prime Minister, Winston Churchill, announced that the "Battle of Britain" was about to begin. The "Blitz," an abbreviation of the German word Blitzkrieg (lightning war), described a period of intense bombing by the Luftwaffe, the German Air Force. Although a number of other British cities also suffered severe bomb damage, "The Blitz" usually refers to the London Blitz, since it was the most heavily attacked city in Britain.

There weren't many redeeming features about World War II from a Londoner's point of view, but it did allow its citizens to demonstrate their indomitable spirit. I look back at those times with great pride.

I may be an ex-Brit, but I'll never be an ex-Londoner.

This is my story. As I remember it. As I lived it. Not some insightful historian's detailed account, but the recollections of a young boy. The memories are all firmly in place. And when nudged, they gush forth. The sounds, sights, and acrid dust of war. The pain and the fear. The uncertainty of everyday living. Or, as it evolved, everyday dying.

Not war in some strange, distant land, but war in my ordinary hometown. In my familiar street. In my old, everyday house.

The memories of those turbulent years run deep. They defined my childhood. They taught me survival. And they taught me the power of humor. Indeed, we made fun of the Nazis as often as we could, and Hitler, Goering, and their goose-stepping henchman lent themselves well to that end. The traitorous Lord Haw-Haw too. Ridicule proved to be a powerful weapon. Unfortunately, it was one of the only weapons we had at the time. At least until the US entered the war in December, 1941.

When I first sat down to write my story, my journey back in time, I realized I had a problem: which language should I use? I was born and educated in London, emigrating to the US when I was twenty-nine. So my mother tongue was English. My father's tongue had a tiny blister on it, so I did as Mama said.

As part of the naturalization process to become an American citizen, I had to learn American. Fortunately, I had five years to achieve this. And I needed all of them. Now, after living in America for the last fifty-five years, I still have language problems. My accent is...well, bastardized at best. Think of it as Amerglish. Or Englican? But I write in American. More or less. In the book, quotations by Brits, are in the language they used, as are titles of British institutions. My own early quotations are also in British English, or more accurately, in the cockney dialect.

"Cockney dialect?" I hear my American friend ask. "What's that?" Well, traditionally, a cockney is defined as a native of East London, born within the sound of Bow Bells. The dialect leans heavily on rhyming slang. The cockneys of my day were typically rough, tough, good-humored members of the working-class. Events of World War II demonstrated their fierce strength and determination under the most challenging of circumstances.

The cockney dialect is a far cry from Stephen Fry's lyrical view, when he says, "The English language is like London: proudly barbaric yet deeply civilised, too, common yet royal, vulgar yet processional, sacred yet profane." Then again, Fry has a way with words. My words often have their way with me.

So I ask my British reader, whoever he is, to forgive me for abandoning my native tongue, and I ask my American reader, if there is one, to be understanding, and cut me some slack. Lots of slack. I need slack.

My first novel, PreMedicated Murder, was published in late 2015. I was nearly eighty-three at the time. At the Florida Authors and Publishers Association's 2016 Book Awards, my entry won awards in two categories: Humor and Adult Fiction Mystery. I thus became an award-winning two-timer, old-timer. I was thrilled, of course. That success encouraged me to extend my late-life writing career. So I did. Hence *The Catcher Goes Awry…and Other Odds and Sods.* And now, book three, *London's Bloody Blitz.*

Following the publication of book number one, a frequent question was: "And what are you working on now?"

I heard myself offering ho-hum replies like: "Well, for my second book…" But whatever followed sounded so…

inadequate. Second book indeed! So I offered a more provocative response. "What am I working now? I'm working on my fourteenth book."

"Really?" was the typical reply. "Impressive."

I had to confess that there was no book Two through Thirteen. My next novel was going to be titled, *My Fourteenth Book*. That would be my second book. I'll call my third *My Fifteenth Book*. If Sue Grafton can have her Alphabet series, why can't I have my Ordinals?

This book, the erstwhile Fifteenth, is divided into chapters; each one deals with a particular feature of the war and my personal involvement in it. A few names have been changed to protect the innocent; others are unchanged. The less innocent. Since the events described took place nearly eighty years ago, most of the people involved have been long gone anyway. As I have, at least from London.

On one level, it's a series of short stories. On another, the episodes all coalesce to form the turbulent six-year period that consumed my boyhood. While the events I describe are in chronological order, there is considerable overlap among them. Some experiences were relatively brief, just hours, days, or weeks long; others, like rationing, spanned much of the duration of the war.

In addition to WWII action, I touch on life in old London, especially the area known as the East End. And

I could scarcely ignore two social issues that significantly impacted my life: the British class structure and corporal punishment. In reliving those memories, splashes of venom inevitably nudge the humor aside. There's also the discovery of sex, but don't let that overly excite you. Remember, I was just a kid at the time.

Preceding each chapter is a PreScript, a brief comment that, in various forms, leads us into the theme of the subject at hand. Following each chapter, there's a PostScript. This is mostly additional information that, at the time, I wasn't privy to. It expands and updates the story that precedes it. In some cases, I had access to original documents, including official British, American, and German communications. Many of these only became available in recent years.

Mark Twain is generally credited with the notion that "God created war so that Americans would learn geography." So if he's right, a little geography might help in the chapters to come.

Here beginneth the lesson:

The countries of England, Scotland, and Wales, together, form Great Britain. The island of Ireland, separated from Great Britain by the Irish Sea, is divided into two parts: Northern Ireland, not surprisingly located at the northern end, and the independent Republic of Ireland, generally known as Ireland. Or Eire. And yes, that's in the south. Great Britain and Northern Island, together, form the

United Kingdom of Great Britain and Northern Ireland. The United Kingdom. The UK. Its people are called British, Britons, or more popularly, especially in the US, Brits. London is both the capital of England and the capital of the United Kingdom. Many now believe that Britain is no longer Great, and that the Kingdom is no longer United. All I can say is that things were fine when I left.

To many an arrogant Londoner, it's all much simpler. The UK is divided into two parts: London, and outside London. As I learned from many non-Londoners during my wartime travels, however, not every Brit embraces this concept. Or this conceit.

It's worth keeping in mind that Great Britain is just twenty miles from France, across the English Channel. Dover to Calais. By mid-1940, Germany had occupied France, thus effectively shortening its distance from Britain. The English Channel proved to be a most important stretch of water, making a German invasion of the UK that much more of a challenge. It was arguably the ultimate difference between victory and defeat.

Since my story is not intended to be a scholarly work, I cite few references. But I must mention one source that provided me with fascinating input: The British Broadcasting Corporation's audio clips. The BBC, a public service organization, is headquartered in London. We call her Auntie; no one really knows why. The well organized, archived records of the BBC allowed me access to a fascinating collection of audio clips. Hearing those for the first time in decades was a totally unexpected experience. After all these years, I listened to the wailing of a genuine air raid siren warning of an imminent attack. I'd heard these sirens innumerable times over the years, in all kinds of radio and television programs and movies. But they just didn't seem to grab me. The BBC's audio clip did. This was different. Evocative. Frighteningly real. Because it was. I reacted in a way that astonished me: my heart began to pound; I began to perspire; nausea swept through me. The sirens no longer triggered my curiosity. I now only reacted to the anticipated fear of what was to come. Truly a psychophysiological response.

More uplifting was the recorded roar of my favorite Royal Air Force fighter plane, the Spitfire, as it climbed, twisted, and raced across the sky to do battle with the invading fighters and bombers of the German Luftwaffe. What a sight. What a sound. I remember both so well. And the recordings of the live broadcast speeches of Prime Minister Winston Churchill? They too were memories to remember.

It was the Battle of Britain and the London Blitz, all over again. And I was back there in the middle of it.

1

War!
PreScript

"The object of war is not to die for your country
But to make the other bastard die for his."

George S. Patton
General, US Army

Right on, Georgie.

War!

Script

And in the beginning, God created the heavens and the earth. And World War II. Maybe that's why I'm godless.

It was one of those memorable moments that stay indelibly etched in one's mind—even that of a young boy. I had no idea of the seriousness of the occasion, but the adults around me obviously did. I could sense their apprehension. I could feel the heaviness of the moment. It was palpable.

At 11:15 am on September 3, 1939, the British Prime Minister, Neville Chamberlain, addressed the nation:

"I am speaking to you from the Cabinet Room at 10 Downing Street. This morning the British Ambassador in Berlin handed the German Government a final note stating that, unless we hear from them by 11 o'clock that they were prepared at once to withdraw their troops from Poland, a state of war would exist between us. I have to tell you now that no such undertaking has been received, and consequently this country is at war with Germany."

Later that day, France joined Britain in its declaration of war. Canada, Australia, and New Zealand subsequently followed suit.

If I'd have had the chance, I'd have said a few things to Mr. Chamberlain. Like:

"'Ere, just a minute, Mister. When you say, 'The country is at war,' j'ou mean kids too? Well, you should know somefin.' It ain't a good idea. See, me birfday is comin' up in a couple o' weeks. September 29. That's Michaelmas Day. I'll be seven, and I got plans for that day. Big plans. I 'ope this war o' yours is over by then. I'm gettin' a chemistry set, and I'm gonna be busy doin' speriments. If you want, I fink I could make some gunpowder. You could then 'ave someone chuck it at 'itler. At'll take care of 'im."

Well, at least it was a plan. And it would have been more effective than any the British government apparently had at the time.

As if he was deliberately ignoring my concerns, the British monarch, King George VI, added "…I now call my people at home and my peoples across the seas…to stand calm, firm and united in this time of trial. The task will be hard. There may be dark days ahead, and war can no longer be confined to the battlefield."

Mmm. Maybe I should 'ave a chat wiv 'im too.

Meanwhile, the telephone in Franklin Roosevelt's bedroom at the White House rang at 2:50 a.m. on the first day of September. He was informed that "Adolf Hitler's bombing planes were dropping death all over Poland." World War II had begun.

Fully expecting that German bombing would result in significant civilian deaths, the government instituted an aggressive evacuation program, primarily for children. Their evacuation from cities across Britain took place in several waves. The first was on September 1, 1939, the day Germany invaded Poland, and two days before we formally declared war. Over a three day period, one-and-a-half million evacuees were sent to safe havens throughout the British countryside.

"Safe?" Well, that was a relative term. Safer than London, maybe, but not safe enough for the people who mattered. Many of the wealthier, privileged Brits had already sent their children abroad, to the US and to British Commonwealth countries like Canada, Australia, and New Zealand. And this issue became quite a bone of intention. Contention too!

We were warned of air raids to come—but there were none. For months on end. We had rationing, gas masks, blackouts, and lots of practice taking shelter. But we waited. And waited. It was strangely anticlimactic. By now, it was being called the phoney war, and the major issue of the day seemed to be whether the word was spelled phoney, the English way, or US-style, phony. The press called it "Sitzkrieg," "the sitting war," a play on the word Blitzkrieg.

Despite the relative calm on land, war on the high seas was very evident: a number of British ships were torpedoed within hours of the start of the conflict.

Nevertheless, a way of life dies hard. Early on in the war, the best of British good manners were still in evidence. Attitudes to our German adversaries remained noticeably civilized. In April, 1940, a German Heinkel bomber crashed in the countryside just outside London; its crew members were all killed in the crash. They were laid to rest in the local cemetery, and wreathes with messages of sympathy were displayed on the coffins.

And then Dunkirk happened.

My mother's birthday was May 26. We were sitting in the kitchen, enjoying tea and cake to celebrate the occasion. But instead of my mother taking center stage, the conversation was all about Dunkirk. I'd never heard of the place before, but learned that it was just a few miles from the English coast on the other side of the Channel. In France. As history tells us, May 26 was the day the massive evacuation of British troops from Dunkirk began. The older brother of my friend Tony was among them; he survived. Alan's father didn't. It suddenly seemed as if everyone was talking about Dunkirk. Especially Churchill.

Stories of how barbaric the Germans were, began to dominate the news. So my pals and I felt obliged to modify our regular game of Cowboys and Indians, where the cowboy had the toy gun, and the Indian, a rubber dagger. We switched to Nazis and Brits—but we had a problem: we didn't know what a Nazi looked like. And anyway, no one wanted to be one. So we quickly returned to Cowboys and Indians. Come to think of it, we'd never seen a cowboy or an Indian either. Not in the flesh, anyway.

A few short months later, Luftwaffe air raids on London had begun in earnest. The first of the fifty-seven consecutive nights of bombing began on September 7, 1940. The Blitzkrieg continued until May, 1941.

The initial bombing raids were centered on the East End of London, an area that lies east of the Roman and medieval walls of the City of London and north of the River Thames. Right where I lived.

The relentless killing of tens of thousands of Londoners inevitably and drastically changed the civility of the Brits.

As young as I was, I could recognize the change. While the Londoner's lighter side always bubbled to the surface, the undercurrent of their grit and determination ran deep and strong. We could smile and kid around, but still be ready to fight to the death. As many of my fellow Londoners did.

The conflict would prove to be unending—or so it seemed to be: phase one of the London Blitz was behind us, but lots more war was still to come. Some of us would survive; many wouldn't. I had neither the time nor the understanding to worry about that. I had a job to do. I was busy making gunpowder. Sulfur, 10%; Charcoal, 15%; Saltpeter, 75%. A simple goal with a noble purpose. After all, I'd promised that to the Prime Minister. And a promise was a promise.

War!

PostScript

Why was the East End a primary bombing target? Two reasons: its proximity to the important docklands area of London that was a hub for imports and storage of vital goods, and because that section of the city was densely populated. The result would be high civilian casualties.

It's also possible that Germany saw the area to be quite dispensable in its long-range strategic thinking. It was long speculated that Hitler planned to use Oxford, or perhaps Cambridge, as a site for the future headquarters of the Nazi occupation forces in Britain. More recently, just a few years ago, in fact, new German documents came to light suggesting that Hitler's UK headquarters would be in the sleepy town of Bridgworth in Shropshire, near the Welsh border. In any event, all of these locations were significantly distant from the death and destruction the Nazis inflicted upon the East End of London.

And what of Nazi Germany? How did they explain their invasion of Poland? How did they react to England's Declaration of War? Outrageously, that's how.

The German army began publishing a biweekly magazine in 1937. This article is the first reporting on the German invasion of Poland. They claim that Hitler was completely innocent, and indeed that Poland had plans to take over most of Germany!

Here's what they said:

"Why are we fighting?

Because we were forced into it by England and its Polish friends...England and France began the war in 1939 because they feared that in two or three years Germany would be militarily stronger and harder to defeat. The deepest roots of this war are in England's old claim to rule the world and Europe in particular...

The English wanted this war in the crazy hope that it was their last chance to stop Germany's growing strength... Rather than encouraging Poland to accept the Führer's generous proposals...they encouraged it to let the deadline pass, thereby providing a reason for war. The Führer felt obliged to strike back only after Polish troops had crossed the German border at several places. The German fight is a defensive fight. We fight because we were forced to fight by the insults and demands against us, (and) because of the brutal suppression of ethnic Germans in Poland.

What are we fighting for?

We are fighting for our most valuable possession: our freedom. We are fighting for our land and our skies. We are fighting so that our children will not be slaves of foreign rulers. We know the English…We know that we will be slaves if we do not win and we know that the goal of England's policy…is to subject Germany to its will. We are fighting for Germany's freedom and for Germany's right to be a people that has all it needs to preserve its national existence. The Führer made unprecedented offers for peace and understanding to those who are now fighting against Germany. His attempts were scornfully rejected because they wanted this fight…We are fighting to save our children from the unbearable threats of the Western democracies, driven by envy and hatred. We are fighting for a happy future in a free Germany in a peaceful Europe."

German Propaganda Archive
"Warum und wofür?" [Why and For What?]
Die Wehrmacht [The German Army], 3 (1939, Nr. 19), p. 2.

Of course! It's all so clear now. Hitler obviously did all he could to find a peaceful solution to the problems that Britain and France inflicted upon him.

2

Winnie

PreScript

"I think a curse should rest on me because I love this war.
I know it's smashing and shattering the lives of thousands
every moment...and yet...I can't help it...I enjoy every
second of it."

Winston Churchill
Letter to a Friend

Blood-thirsty sod, wasn't he. Hard to believe that he was
nominated for the Nobel *Peace* Prize!

Winnie

Script

In May, 1940, losing his support in Government, and citing ill health, Neville Chamberlain resigned from the premiership. Few accepted the ill-health excuse, till he died of cancer some months later.

Well, can you really believe a politician?

King George appointed Winston Churchill. Apparently, several other prominent politicians were considered, but no one else was keen to take the job. Churchill was. It was wartime, and our new leader was finally where he was destined to be. In his element. And in ours, too. The Russians dubbed Churchill, the Bulldog. The British Bulldog, of course. But we, the people, affectionately came to know him as Winnie.

No aristocratic lightweight, Winston Leonard Spencer-Churchill was born in Blenheim Palace, the residence of his grandfather, the Seventh Duke of Marlborough. His father was the Duke's third son, Lord Randolph Churchill.

Despite his "breeding distance" from the masses, Churchill was an inspiring leader, and was accepted by much of the country. He was certainly admired by my family. Especially my mother. And so he figures prominently in these pages.

I saw Winnie once. Up close. He watched while many of our neighbors and friends were digging through rubble, looking for other neighbors and friends. Our leader was touring the East End after we'd endured a particularly brutal bombing raid the night before. My friend Tony, or as I might have called him at the time, "me mucker," thought that Winnie would probably invite us to join him for elevenses (mid-morning tea and cookies) or afternoon tea. Instead, I think he tried to flick his cigar ash on me. Then again, maybe he just waved at me while holding his cigar.

A few weeks later, it was the royals turn: King George VI and Queen Elizabeth, The Queen Mother, came to check on us. They didn't invite us to join them for anything either. But I did eventually meet the Queen Mother. A number of years later, I graduated from the University of London, and was presented to her Majesty in her capacity as Chancellor of the University. I was tempted to remind her that she still owed me tea and cookies!

To any Londoner who was around during the early forties, Churchill's extraordinary wartime broadcasts will surely be somewhere at the top of their more vivid memories. He claimed that all he did was to give voice to the national mood of defiance: "The people's will was resolute and remorseless, I only expressed it. I had the luck to be called upon to give the roar."

And roar he did.

We came to depend on and faithfully follow the BBC and Churchill. To us, the BBC *was* Churchill. When the great man spoke, we listened. When the announcement was made that Prime Minister Winston Churchill was about to address the nation, my mother immediately stood to attention. She didn't actually do that, of course, but it sure felt as if she did. If one can sit to attention, then she at least did that—literally. As we all had to. Armed with dictation paper and writing implements, she waited for Him to speak. As a one-time executive secretary, before there was such a title, my mother took great pride in her unusually fast and accurate shorthand and typing. And her handwriting was a work of art. To keep her shorthand hand in, she recorded every one of Churchill's addresses to the nation. I bet she even captured his every lisp and stammer.

I was obliged to stay quiet during these times. So was the dog. And if I didn't actually listen to the latest news, I at least had to allow my mother to carry out her self-appointed task with no distractions. I have no idea what she did with her record of his speeches, but I well remember how intently she listened to the sonorous tones of the great man's inimitable voice. It wasn't only what he said, but how he said it. That shakes a few wartime memories loose.

Winnie

PostScript

My mother would have been proud to know that one of her grandsons, my middle son, had the same birthday as Churchill, November 30. And at the time of my son's birth, they both looked remarkably alike: round-faced and wrinkled. Only one of them smoked cigars and drank Scotch.

Churchill proved to be extremely popular in the United States. Perhaps even more so than he was in the UK. His mother, Jennie Jerome, was the daughter of an American financier, and that probably helped. In any event, Winnie achieved that rare distinction of becoming an honorary citizen of the United States.

Postwar analysis of Churchill's actions and behavior, point to depression. Possibly manic depression. He called it his "black dog." Personally, I think he was just worried that the war threatened his continuing supply of good booze and premium cigars.

Makes sense that being deprived would be enough to drive anyone into depression. Or to drink.

3

Auntie

PreScript

John Charles Walsham Reith, Baron Reith, the BBC's founding father, was a British Broadcasting executive who established the tradition of independent public service broadcasting in the United Kingdom. He was the Director-General of the British Broadcasting Corporation created under a Royal Charter. We called the BBC "Auntie." Dunno why. Auntie Knows Best, perhaps?

Reith had always disliked Winston Churchill—loathed him, in fact. In turn, Churchill had only contempt for Reith. They had different ideas about the function of the BBC. Keith insisted it remained independent; Churchill wanted to use it as a government voice. His voice.

Meanwhile, Churchill referred to the puritanical Scot who towered over him as "That Wuthering Height," and wrote: "I absolutely hate him."

These two giant egos were destined to collide. Churchill never forgave the BBC for what he saw as the censorship of his views. Years later, he would exact his revenge.

After the war, Reith remarked: "A whole lot of people could have done it better and more cheaply."

Really? I wonder who he had in mind?

And so, Keith played his part, but Churchill inherited the glory.

Auntie
Script

Even as a small boy, I could appreciate how important the British Broadcasting Corporation, the BBC, was to the general British public during the war; it was a major wartime lifeline—however filtered the news may have been. We had newspapers, of course, but the radio always seemed to be the primary source of news and entertainment. There were no television transmissions, and anyway, we didn't own a television set. Not many did. We also had only one wireless. And few stations: the BBC's Home Service for news, and the Light Programme for, well, the lighter stuff.

The most important programs, at least in our house, were the frequent news programs. For the first few months after war was declared, we heard from Prime Minister, Neville Chamberlain. And then, for the remainder of the six years, we were under the leadership of The Right Honourable,

Winston Churchill. Winnie. A strong and inspiring leader, to be sure. Especially in our household.

While the radio wasn't much fun for kids, a few comedy programs helped: one of my favorites was *It's That Man Again*. The belittlement of Hitler and his stooges always made them seem less frightening.

By the way, did you know that it was Thomas Jefferson who first coined the word, "belittle?" I didn't, until recently. You just might be deriving unexpected benefits from reading this stuff!

Quite coincidentally, the show's frequent use of acronyms was arguably a forerunner of today's texting style. The program, *It's That Man Again*, was better known as *ITMA*. And among other popular acronyms the show introduced was *TTFN*, "ta-ta for now." a phrase that's still in use today; well, I use it, anyway.

Unless I was tucked away in an air raid shelter somewhere, at some point during the evening, especially if they noticed me yawning (dammit!), I was told it was time for bed. If I felt it was unfairly early, and of course it usually was, I'd sneak my crystal set under the blanket and listen to more BBC broadcasts, or to any other radio signals I could get.

I should probably explain what a crystal set, or crystal radio, is. Especially for the younger folk. Less than eighty is "younger." Much younger, actually.

A crystal set is the simplest of radio receivers. I built my own from a coil of wire, a thin wire detector called a "cat's whisker," a crystal of lead sulfide, and a cheap pair of earphones. There are no batteries or electrical power involved, and every kid ought to put a crystal set together—both for the fun of it and as a fascinating learning experience. I remember picking up both the BBC and occasionally a foreign language transmission that I knew was from Mars. Unfortunately, I didn't speak Martian, so I never knew what they were saying. Probably plotting against earthlings. Sneaky bastards! Maybe I was listening to the American Forces Network; those people had strange accents too.

The AFN began transmitting from London in mid-1943. While their programs were clearly directed to American Service men and women, many Brits happily tuned in too. They were obviously not intended for British listeners, or they'd have been called "programmes" not "programs." But I liked them, and became familiar with many of the famous bands and singers of that period. In fact, when D-Day arrived on June 6, 1944, I was sure that the "D" stood for Doris, and that D-Day was Doris Day, the popular singer. Perhaps some kind of code. Well, I was only eleven.

Another offering from the BBC that almost fell into the comedy category, was a weekly address, to the British nation, by the traitor, William Joyce. From Germany. We all had fun with his pro-German propaganda broadcasts. His opening, that sounded like: "Jairmany Calling. Jairmany Calling," said in a posh, toffee-nosed git accent, led to his nickname of Lord Haw-Haw. We laughed at everything he said. A good example of fighting 'em with ridicule.

Nobody told me what happened to Lord Haw-Haw at the end of the war. It was said that he fled to South America with all the other prominent Nazi bastards.

Auntie
PostScript

But not so, apparently. Lord Haw-Haw didn't flee anywhere. It was much later when I found out exactly what happened to the traitorous bastard.

William Joyce was born in New York. He moved with his English mother and Irish-American father to England when he was a teenager. As a Nazi sympathizer, he fled to Germany at the beginning of the war and became a broadcaster for Goebbel's Propaganda Ministry. He transmitted a weekly program directed at the Brits throughout the whole of the war, spewing lots of anti-British venom. "Fake News." And who could take anyone by the name of Lord Haw-Haw seriously?

Captured by the British, Joyce stood trial for treason. The court denied his claim of American citizenship because he held a British passport. He was found guilty and hanged.

I guess we had the last ha-ha, Haw-Haw.

4

The Iron Lady
PreScript

The East End's row-home streets of prewar London were busy places: no cars, but lots of street activity.

There were scheduled deliveries of coal and, since refrigerators were essentially non-existent, milk. If left outside, glass bottles sealed by cardboard discs, invited pigeons to peck their way through the cardboard and enjoy the creamy, unhomogenized upper layers. We had what was left: skim milk. Nature Made.

We had a steady stream of street vendors. The ice cream man peddled his wares, and pedaled his wares, literally, on a tricycle. He offered a wide variety of flavors, especially vanilla. Actually, only vanilla. Wrapped in paper, it sold for a penny; he'd sell you half for a ha'penny. Knife grinders and tinkers constantly did the rounds, and a rag-and-bone man would seemingly collect anything. Or anyone?

There were two other street activities that quickly disappeared from the scene soon after war was declared; one was my special favorite. At dusk, a lamplighter would arrive, by bicycle, and would light a nearby gas lamp. I loved to see the flickering flame. At dawn, he'd return to snuff it out. As soon as blackouts began, and street lights were left unlit, we saw neither gaslights nor, as the song has it, "The old lamplighter of long, long ago." I often wondered what happened to him. He always waved a friendly "hello" to me.

The other tradesman we frequently heard from, in times of peace but never again during the war, was the man who traveled the streets by horse and cart, calling out, or occasionally singing: "Any old iron? Any old iron? Any, any, any, old iron?"

The collection of old iron, and indeed, new iron, quickly became a key element in the overall war effort. It was carried out on a huge scale, and really pissed off sweet, old Mrs. Cooper.

Here's why.

The Iron Lady
Script

As part of the war effort during the 1940s, iron gates and or-
namental railings around houses, buildings, garden squares,
and parks throughout London were removed for recycling
into munitions. There's evidence to suggest, and no surprise
to me, that railings were removed "more enthusiastically"
from working-class districts than from around the houses
of the wealthy and socially influential.

Over a million tons of metal were collected, including the
few iron bars in front of dear old Mrs. Cooper's little house.
Mrs. C., who was indeed both dear and old, lived at 12
British Street, the house next door ours. "Old?" Back then,
sixty was old. Surrounded by young families, the Widow
Cooper was everyone's grandma: a Disneyesque character,
she was a five-foot tall, roly-poly, white-haired, charmer.
The majority of the birds we had in London were pigeons
and sparrows. If we'd have had just one colored bird, then

in true Disney style, it would have been perched on Mrs. Cooper's shoulder. But we didn't have any such bird. So it wasn't. You get the picture—even if it's not in color.

Mrs. C. was always ready to share her home-made cookies ("biscuits," as she called them) with any kid who said "Please," often teasing them a little in the process. And they eventually learned to mumble their "Fanks" too. Sadly, when rationing came into our lives, the ingredients for cookies were rarely available. So her cookie offerings gradually came to a halt. I think she was more upset by her inability to give than we were by our inability to receive.

One of her passions was the nurturing of her front garden: a narrow strip of flowers that surrounded a small concrete rectangle. A wrought iron fence protected it from children, balls, dogs, and to a degree, the elements. She viewed her fence as her protector and looked after it with unusual care and affection. Following every rainfall, and London certainly had its unfair share, she'd wipe off all the watermarks, leaving the metal shining. At Christmas time, she would decorate the railings with tinsel, and on the reigning monarch's birthday, she'd attach a row of tiny Union Jacks (the British flag) to the top of each vertical bar.

Before they removed Mrs. Cooper's railings, there was... an incident. In the interest of full disclosure, I should elaborate.

I was in her front yard digging up a patch of earth for her new plantings. There was tuppence (two pence) in it for me, so this was a big money assignment.

I was deep in thought, wondering what to spend this windfall on, when a kid who was on everyone's "Least Popular" list walked by. Euripides Smith. Yes, you're right. Not a name you'd expect for an EastEnder; his mother apparently had high hopes for her son's academic future. Some adults called him Euri, but since he had curly, ginger hair, we called him Ginger. He was, of course, "Ginger Smiff" to a cockney.

In addition to defending his unusual name and his unusual hair, Ginger had a couple of other problems to deal with. The poor boy's ears stuck out; I mean really stuck out. Must have been close to forming right angles with his head. His two front teeth bordered on the buck, and while he was about our age, he was much taller and skinnier than the rest of us. All this obviously provided us with plenty of opportunities for cruel comments. For the record, he also had a nose that was straight out of a plastic surgeon's "Catalogue of the Ideal," and eyes that movie stars might envy—but no kid was going to dwell on the good bits. In addition to his physical appearance, or perhaps because of it, Ginger had a few behavioral problems. First, he was something of a bully: he took pleasure in pushing us hard whenever we were within reach. He also liked to poke his tongue out and make a funny face. No one told him that he didn't need to make a funny face; the poor sod already had one. His taunting, mocking *Nah Nah Na Nah Nah* sung repetitively was always annoying.

Seeing me at work, he pushed his head up against the vertical iron bars of Mrs. Cooper's railing, looked hard at what I was doing, and chided, "*That's a terrible job.*"

I was defensive. "No it ain't."

"Yes it is. Look at it. It's all crooked."

"No it bloody well ain't."

"Yes it bloody well is."

"Lemme see," I said, going round to his side of the railing.

"Worst bit o' diggin' I've ever seen," he said.

If Mrs. Cooper 'ears 'im, my big tupp'ny deal could fall through, I thought.

The fear of that possibility gave me unusual courage—and strength. While Ginger continued to stare through the vertical bars, explicitly finding more faults with my work, I went behind him, said "You bastard!" and pushed his head forward as hard as I could. To my surprise, his ears flattened out, and with a soft popping sound, his head easily slipped through the bars.

I went round to the digging side of the fence, and looked at Ginger's isolated head with great pleasure. *Good,* I thought. *He was where he should be: behind bars.* And he'd stopped his irritating *Nah Nah Nahing.*

Understandably, Ginger immediately began trying to pull his head back through the bars. He couldn't. His prominent ears didn't allow it. Squashed close to his head they allowed him to go forward, but they opened up when he tried to reverse. The more he tried to pull back, the redder his face became. He started to cry. Then scream. I reacted to both his obvious panic and to my guilt, and tried hard to push his head back through the bars. I couldn't. I went back around to the body side and tried pulling. No use; his ears held firm.

"'*elp. 'elp*," he screamed as loudly as he could.

Nothing more I can do, I thought, so I went back to my digging; my tuppence was still on the line.

Ginger's desperate cries began to attract adult attention. Two neighbors rushed over and tried to maneuver him out of his predicament. They squeezed and pushed and twisted and pulled. I was a little apprehensive.

Suppose 'is 'ead comes off, I thought. *It would be my fault. My mother would be really mad at me.*

But his head didn't come off, although from his screams you'd never know it. By now, his face was the same color as his hair. I'd never seen a ginger face before.

One of the adults had the bright idea of spreading butter on his ears to facilitate his release. That proved to be a waste of time, and more significantly, a waste of rationed butter.

A third neighbor joined the fray and announced that she'd contacted the emergency rescue people, and they were on their way. They arrived fifteen minutes later.

"Well now, young man," a reassuring rescuer said calmly to Ginger. "And just how did you get yourself into this fix?"

Ginger yelled, "'*e did it*!" Since I was standing behind him, he twisted his neck and body trying hard to point at me. Fortunately, no one could follow who the "'e" was. So I just stood there, looking innocent.

They managed to free Ginger by prizing the two bars apart. I was relieved to see that his head was still attached to his body. Ginger was probably even more relieved.

Euripides Smith wasn't quite as good as new, but arguably good enough. His ears were still attached; he was in one piece. They cleaned him up, and said "Okay, sonny. You're fine now. Off you go."

Ginger turned to go back home, glaring at me with an implied, *I'm gonna git you.* But somehow there wasn't much conviction in the threat.

"See you Ginge," I said, and went back to my digging.

I finished my job, collected my tuppence, and was never bullied by Ginger again.

Can't remember what I spent the moolah on.

Some time after the removal of her railings, London experienced a light snowfall; Mrs. Cooper's iron fence would have kept this to no more than a dusting. The residual iron stumps, however, failed to hold back the accumulation of the inch of snow that fell.

Never before had anyone seen sweet Mrs. Cooper so angry. Holding a small spade out towards me, Mrs. Cooper said, "I'll give you thruppence to shovel out my snow."

Wow, I thought. *Thruppence. Three pence. That's three, full-size ice-creams!*

And that reminds me of the time, many years later, but still many years ago, I arrived in Dublin and met a friend in a pub. I was looking forward to a glass of my favorite Irish beer.

"How much is Guinness these days?" I asked.

"Three pints to the pound," he said, as if were an exchange rate.

That was then. What is it now? Three pounds to the pint? You wish. *I* wish. More like five.

But as I was saying, or rather, as Mrs. Cooper was saying, "Thruppence to shovel…."

Since I'd have gladly done it for a penny, I jumped at the offer. "Sure. I'll do it right now." And did. I knocked on her door to collect my fee.

Mrs. Cooper came out, looked around, nodded, and wearing an odd kind of smile, said, "Okay. But I'm not going to pay you. What are you going to do about that?"

I knew it! She still remembered the "pickle incident." And she was punishing me for it. Yeah, I know. I have to explain that.

I was a relatively shy kid, and I knew that Mrs. Cooper had a soft spot for me. She'd often send me on errands, and supplement my nonexistent allowance with the reward of a penny here and a penny there. A few days earlier, she'd sent me to the corner grocery store to buy a pickle.

"Pick me a plump one from the barrel," she instructed. Fifteen minutes later, she took the small bag from me withdrawing what was, in essence, the shrunken skin of a pickle. I could scarcely tell her that I'd bitten off the end of the pickle and sucked out its inners. She was suspicious, of course, but quietly accepted the emaciated offering, perhaps as yet another wartime hardship she had to endure. She frowned, said nothing, and gave me a penny for my effort. She never asked me to buy her another pickle—ever again.

So that's it, I thought. Pickle punishment. I'll never collect that thruppence now. I slowly started to shovel the snow back again.

She chuckled, and said, "No, don't do that. I'll give you your thruppence."

I ignored her, and kept shoveling until the snow was all back in its place.

She sighed. "All right. I'll give you sixpence to take it all away."

I again shoveled the snow into the street, but this time collected a tanner; that sixp'ny bit was a fortune!

In addition to the gathering and recycling of metals, paper was another material deemed relevant to the war effort and mandated for collection. The national response to this was impressive: in 1943 alone, 600 million books were recycled. I was one of the many thousands of British kids who was co-opted to participate.

Germany had its "Hitler Youth" program, where eleven and twelve-year-old boys were armed and sent into battle. British kids were asked to collect books. Since we won the bloody war, surely that proved that the pen was mightier than the sword—even if we did convert the written word back into military materiel.

And so we enthusiastically set about our appointed task, where the more books we collected the higher the rank we could achieve. Finding books in a relatively book-less neighborhood, however, was challenging. After much effort, I was still one short of my goal.

Reluctantly, I knew I had to give up my prized possession for the cause: a comic book compendium that I'd kept hidden under the bed away from unscrupulous book thieves. But that gut-wrenching sacrifice did it! That was the book that swept me to glory, earning me the prize I had long coveted: a small, round, cardboard badge, stamped, "Captain." An attached loop of string completed the award. My mother was proud.

As I reflect on these events long past, it's sobering to realize that without my contribution, 1943 would have seen the collection of only 599,999,999 books. It could have cost us the war!

And another thing: whatever happened to that cardboard badge?

The Iron Lady
PostScript

What Mrs. Cooper never knew was that the eventual disposition of all the iron collected during the war would remain something of a mystery. Indeed, it's been a matter of speculation for decades. The Public Records Office insists that most of the official records have been shredded. Yeah sure!

It's been reported that only a quarter of the vast amount of iron collected may have been put to war-related use. Many sources suggest that, since the program appeared to be a unifying effort for the country, and of great propaganda value, especially for the benefit of US politicians reluctant to enter the war, the government allowed the program to continue. It's now generally believed that the bulk of the collected metal was dumped, much of it in the Thames Estuary.

Sadly, even today, London remains littered with stumps remaining from the removed railings. Mrs. Cooper would not be pleased.

A few months before the end of the war, we lost Mrs. Cooper. No, not to poor health, or to an air raid, the dear lady finally decided to join her daughter who had a small farm in Glamorgan, Wales. While there, she apparently befriended a German prisoner of war who had been assigned to work on her daughter's farm. Following Germany's surrender and the repatriation of their POWs, Mrs. Cooper adopted the young soldier, but only after he agreed to replace the iron railings missing from around her daughter's house.

Lady Margaret Thatcher, British Prime Minister, 1979-1990, was given the nickname "Iron Lady" early in her career. The epithet has since become a generic descriptor for strong-willed female politicians.

In her own way, Mrs. Cooper was also a strong-willed lady. Her commitment to the preservation of the country's iron railings made her an Iron Lady of another kind.

Rest in peace, Mrs. C.

5

The ARP, not the AARP
PreScript

The ARP, Britain's World War II Air Raid Precaution Service, was created in 1937 to protect civilians during wartime. Don't confuse it with AARP, formerly the American Association of Retired Persons, founded in 1958: ARP wardens didn't have the benefits of reduced hotel rates.

Precaution

Definition: a measure taken in advance to prevent something dangerous, unpleasant, or inconvenient from happening.

Example: "He had taken the precaution of seeking legal advice."

Informal: contraception. Example: "We never took precautions."

And of special survival importance:

"If you see us running,
Try to keep up."

The Bomb Squad

I was six years old. I'd never heard the word "Precaution" before the war. I came to understand it within the context of "Air Raid Precaution." Its use in contraception was never explained to me.

The ARP, not the AARP
Script

An important component of preserving and protecting London life during the Blitz was the role of the Air Raid Precaution service. The ARP, subsequently a part of a broader Civil Defence program, consisted mostly of volunteer wardens. My father, too old and unfit for active duty, was one. He wore an armband and a tin hat (Britspeak for a steel helmet) with a "W" on the front. I remember being deeply impressed by his "uniform," and quietly longed to join the ARP myself. I didn't know exactly what he did—I just wanted one of those hats! My father made me one out of newspaper, but it just wasn't the same.

A warden's duties were broad: sound the air raid sirens, rescue people from bomb-damaged properties, administer first-aid, keep people away from unexploded bombs, report on fires and looting, supervise people entering and leaving air raid shelters, ensure that people carried their gas masks and knew how to use them, enforce the blackout, and supervise the warden messenger service. In an air raid attack, they were understandably kept busy.

There were nearly one-and-a-half million men and women serving as ARP wardens. Being in the streets during an air raid, guarding unexploded bombs, and rescuing people and animals from bomb-damaged houses, was a high-risk occupation. My father was badly injured pulling children from rubble while debris was still falling. They said he was lucky: broken bones didn't raise too many eyebrows.

Effectively, and for the longest time, the front line of the war for Londoners was London itself. And at the front of that frontline were the ARP wardens.

Of all the ARP activities, it was the messenger service that particularly excited me. Young boys, typically 14 to 18 were needed as messengers. Since telephone lines were often down, it was frequently necessary for volunteer boys to carry messages from wardens to their control centers, using their bicycles. That was the job that I wanted. I had a bike, and I could pedal super fast. I really wanted to be a Royal Air Force Spitfire pilot, but thought I could be a messenger until I was old enough to fly. And messengers got to wear a real tin hat bearing an "M." They were issued an armband, too. I knew that I was too young at seven, but as the war raged on, year after year, and I reached ten, then eleven, I became increasingly more impatient to get in on the action. Unfortunately, I also had to grow into the hat. For the smaller than average kid that I was, that proved to be yet another obstacle I had to overcome. By the time the war in Europe was over, in May, 1945, I was still just twelve. And the tin hat still didn't fit. No messenger service for me. I felt cheated.

The objective of the blackout was to allow no light to be seen that could help enemy planes locate bombing targets. Heavy curtains were used to prevent houses and businesses from showing even a sliver of light. Street lights were switched off; traffic lights and vehicle headlights were masked to deflect their beams downward; even flashlights were limited in size.

ARP wardens were responsible for the rigorous enforcement of the blackout. A fierce bang on the front door, followed by a stern "Put that light out!" was a frequently heard instruction as the wardens regularly patrolled the streets at night. Unfortunately, and certainly unfairly, their enforcement of the regulation seemed to generate considerable resentment among the rest of us.

While it had its lighter moments, the hardships of the blackout took their toll. Lasting the nearly six years of the war, it probably accounted for more adverse impact on morale than most other quality-of-life sacrifices Londoners had to make. Even more than rationing. And it wasn't just an inconvenience: there were hundreds of road deaths attributable to the blackout, even though traffic speed was limited to twenty miles per hour, and curbs were painted white to help drivers. In the country, cows were splashed with white paint so that drivers could avoid them. A moonless night would leave London totally in the dark, as cars went off the road and pedestrians stumbled about blindly. Add a little fog to the mix, a frequent London phenomenon, and venturing outside became a high-risk undertaking. Accidents by and collisions between pedestrians were common; deaths due to drowning sharply increased.

These were not fun times. But, as I said, they did have their lighter moments. Or in the case I now describe, a light moment.

The story was one told too many times by Warden Dad. He was on duty, walking past the pub at the top of our street, enforcing the blackout. As he was supposed to. The pub door was thrown open, and a happy imbiber staggered out. From the bright light within to the pitch black without. He tried to feel his way to the curb of the road. He couldn't. He pulled out a large flashlight, and duly waved it up and down and around, trying to get his bearings.

"Put that light out!" my father ordered.

The man did, and tried to feel his way to the curb of the road somewhere before him. He couldn't. He stumbled badly and fell heavily. Feeling blood trickling down his leg, he again turned his flashlight on, this time to examine the wound.

"Put that light out!" my father ordered once again.

The man did as he was told, struggled to his feet, turned around, and went back into the pub.

"I'll try again tomorrow morning," he slurred.

On another occasion, soon after an air raid warning had sounded, ARP Dad managed to hustle every one off the street and into an underground shelter. With particular concern for expectant mothers, he called into the shelter doorway: "Is anyone pregnant down there?"

A cockney woman's voice replied: "Give us a chance, love, we've only been 'ere a few minutes." Typical World War II London humor, and my father always enjoyed telling that story. I never understood it.

A few months before the end of the war, the blackout was relaxed a little—to a dim-out. This allowed lighting to the equivalent of moonlight. But without the romance.

The ARP, not the AARP
PostScript

Nearly 7,000 ARP wardens died during the Battle of Britain, while many young boys were killed fulfilling their messenger duties. They were sometimes killed in air raids; at other times in traffic accidents often triggered by the dreaded "blackout."

Further to my father's expectant mother story, the British Government recently banned the use of the term "expectant mother" so as not to offend transgender people. Mothers-to-be must now be referred to as "pregnant people." I don't think my father would have approved.

And for those of you more technologically oriented, an update: the benefits of blackouts against air attack are now largely nullified in the face of a technologically sophisticated enemy. Today, not only are night-vision devices readily available to flight crews, but sophisticated satellite-based and inertial navigation systems enable a static target to be readily found by aircraft and guided missiles.

As I might have said back in my London days: fings ain't wot dey useta be.

6

School Daze

PreScript

There is considerable evidence to show that corporal punishment results in adverse effects on brain development, where spanking results in less gray matter in certain areas of the prefrontal cortex.

On the other hand, much of the Bible, and many religious groups, advocate corporal punishment as a means of "keeping the faith." If that's the case, as some assert, then the absence of corporal punishment leads to atheism.

Given these two outcomes, it follows that, depending on the presence or absence of corporal punishment in their lives, kids will develop into bright atheists or dumb believers.

Mmm.

School Daze
Script

You may think that this chapter is less about the lighter side of the London Blitz and more about its darker side. Perhaps so. I must admit it was sometimes hard to see the fun aspects of injustice and abuse, but, for the most part, I did. I had to. It was my way of surviving. Still is.

Wartime survival meant staying alive; school survival was mostly enduring pain and suffering. While the child abuse issues I describe are largely historic, from what I see of life in Britain today, class abuse is still very much alive.

When Britain and Germany became sworn enemies, again, I was attending our local primary (elementary) school. Located on Malmesbury Road, and demonstrating remarkable acuity and insight, they called it Malmesbury Road Primary School. Founded in 1885, it was one of the newer institutions. I enjoyed my time there and did reasonably well. Not great, just well enough to stay out of trouble. Serious trouble, anyway.

In addition to the war-related hardships we suffered, significant physical punishment in schools was the accepted norm. It wasn't as bad as Charles Dickens description of Victorian England in the nineteenth century, but it was still a far cry from what we'd now consider to be civilized behavior in the treatment of children. In other words, it was often brutal, even sadistic. We tough EastEnders were expected to handle that sort of thing. So I guess we did. And those experiences are the ones that tend to fill my memories.

Primary school corporal punishment took a variety of forms, from relatively mild to health-threatening. Malmesbury Road's Headmistress, Miss Hunt, might glare at us for our indiscretions. It was rumored that if she became really mad she'd sit on a kid. And Miss Hunt was vast. Huge. It's worth noting that many porno websites are dedicated to facesitting; perhaps Miss Hunt was ahead of her time. Ahead of mine, anyway.

Punishment for a serious infraction (Serious? Really?), was a stroke or two, or three, of "the cane" on the outstretched palm of the hand. I still remember the ouch! It was argued that it could be a good route to good behavior—if carried out justly, and with restraint on the teacher's part. But there's the rub: too many of those in power were not restrained. Nor was their punishment just.

Early on in my primary school days, I thought Mr. Pickles was going to be my favorite teacher. Maybe I thought the name was funny. But while the tall, thin, angular-faced Mr. Pickles didn't look particularly friendly, turned out he wasn't. He was, in fact, a man to whom words like "hug" and "cuddle" would be totally alien. Since he often sent me on a lunchtime errand to buy him cigarettes, the Du Maurier brand as I recall, I thought he might at least treat me relatively well in class. Lesson learned. I quickly experienced his special brand of punishment. Once. But it was a once that I still remember.

I had committed my usual classroom crime: talking to another kid. Mr. P. would order us to take turns, and box each other's ears. It sounded funny, initially, until I experienced it. We had to clap our cupped hands with the other boy's head in between. It reminded me of crashing cymbals, except that it was usually followed by a sharp scream. And the reason for the scream? Air is forced into the receiving kid's ears, inflicting intense pain for a few minutes and probably partial hearing loss for a day or two. The first kid would try to be extremely gentle, hoping that he'd receive something equally sparing from the other kid. No way would Mr. Pickles allow that. If we hit too gently, he'd insist we did it again—harder.

I wonder if Mr. Pickles knew that ear-boxing could lead to permanent deafness? Yeah, of course he did, the sick bastard.

By the way, it was possible to identify the chronic misbehavers in Mr. Pickles' class: they were the kids who'd go round saying, "Mm?"

Other teachers exercised the more typical forms of immediate physical punishment: they'd throw things like chalk, blackboard erasers, or books. A pulled ear, or a slap on the back of the head, especially from behind, always jolted us into good…well, better behavior. I took comfort in the fact that the law allowing troublemakers to be boiled alive, was repealed in 1547.

On one occasion Mr. Bell, Tinkle, as we called him, hurled a blackboard eraser at the kid next to me. I was a pretty good outfielder in cricket, so I was able to leap up and catch it before it hit its intended target. For a brief moment, I was tempted to throw it back for an "out." Mr. Bell glared. I walked up to him, handed him the eraser and, smart-arsed sod that I was, said, "Sir, I think you dropped this." He glared again, but said nothing. I knew I was now on his list for retribution. There was no justice. No court of appeal. Just punishment, where "just" means "only." not "fair." And sooner or later, right or wrong, it was to be severe or even cruel punishment. With this kind of training, how could we possibly fear a German invasion? Perhaps this was all part of Churchill's grand plan to prepare us for the event that everyone seemed to expect.

And so we waited for the bombing raids and gas attacks to begin. Meanwhile, we focused on the classroom punishment we routinely experienced. We weren't to know that more barbaric forms of pain and suffering were ahead. Both in the schools and from the skies above. Ignorance can be bliss.

Well before the aerial bombardment of London began, I spent two or three largely halcyon months evacuated to the green of Guildford, in the county of Surrey. I then returned to London's East End, and the norm of wartime life. It was a far cry from the lush English countryside, but it was home. And I no longer had to deal with new forms of school punishment that were even more severe and sadistic. But I'll leave the account of my out-of-London experiences for another chapter.

Over the following three years, air raids went from a possibility to, at times, a nightly certainty. It was a period of survival, Especially for Londoners.

I was, by now, ten years old. With no understanding of its importance, I found myself confronting one of the biggest hurdles in my young life. A hurdle that, Sir Cyril Burt could not have expected me to overcome.

For most Londoners, the highest priority during wartime was survival. That was our assigned task. Inevitably, education was less important. An education in methods of survival went with the times. Education in terms of schooling, however, could wait. I didn't worry too much about fractions, dangling participles, and the music of poetry. At the time I didn't, anyway. But later, when I was nearly eleven and was subjected to the so-called Eleven Plus (11+) examination, my educational level was of paramount importance. Whether it was wartime or not, the impact of the test had lifetime consequences. I didn't know it at the time.

Based on the results of that one test, we would be assigned to a grammar school, or to a non-academic secondary/technical school. There was no chance of being reassigned after the test. No way to move from one educational stream to another. What you were at ten or eleven, was what you would be for the rest of your school life. Consequently, rather than focusing on need or ability, what emerged was fierce competition for places at the prestigious grammar schools. Sadly, those who weren't accepted to grammar schools, the vast majority of kids, were labeled as failures—an absurd and harmful description of any young child.

On reflection, my educational readiness for such an important test left a lot to be desired. Daytime air raids frequently forced us to leave the classroom for air raid shelters. Nighttime raids also meant trips to the shelters, and these were often coupled with significant loss of sleep. Periods of evacuation created other difficulties. Educated and/or wealthier parents ensured that their kids were well prepared. Unfortunately, I'm not sure my relatively uneducated parents ever knew or understood the importance of the test, and in any event, were in no position to help me prepare. And books around the house? We had one: a 1935 horse racing manual. My father liked an occasional "flutter" on the horses—a modest, legal bet with a bookie.

As best I recall, we simply arrived at school one day, and were told that we would take "The Eleven Plus Examination." I still wonder how I spent the night before: was I in an air raid shelter, grabbing a few hours of broken sleep?

Not surprisingly under the circumstances, I later learned that I had come perilously close to being excluded from an academic career. I was initially assigned to a "Special Place" category. A neighbor was sure that this meant I was headed either for a mental health facility, or for a corrective institution. In fact, only because another kid, for whatever reason, had elected not to use his place in grammar school, was I allowed in.

Dammit, without their interference, I could have pursued a practical career—like plumbing. And how many times have I been in a desperate search for help with water leaks over the years? Personal and otherwise.

Somehow, then, I made it to grammar school. Maybe I got more out of that horse racing manual than I realized. While I was "in," my rough, tough street buddies weren't. It's not as if they were told they were better suited to other careers; they just weren't good enough to qualify for grammar school. Sadly, they were forced to regard themselves as failures!

Despite the fact that the war brought us all closer together, old friendships suddenly changed. Even though we continued to live on the same street, I was quickly labeled *persona non grata*, and was left to make new friends at my new school, Coopers' Company's grammar school.

So how did I, a "mis-born" boy of working-class, qualify for grammar school? How could I possibly penetrate the upper strata of academia? To do that, meant that I was in direct conflict with the ultimate arbiter of academic potential during those turbulent years: the evil Cyril Burt. From his extensive research on inherited intelligence, Cyril Burt, a leading British educational psychologist, concluded that the children of the upper classes were innately more intelligent than those of the lower classes. Ironically, it was later discovered that the results and conclusions of Burt's extensive testing were fraudulent. Sadly, the lying bastard was knighted for his work.

Frankly, based on my experiences growing up, being educated, and working in England, I always found that aristocrats were innately *less* intelligent than their non-aristocratic counterparts. In the dog world, it seems much the same: mutts are brighter than thoroughbreds.

Admittedly less grotesque, but causing significant harm nevertheless, Burt's use of twins reminds me of that other twin-happy, twisted sod, the evil Nazi, Herr Doktor Josef Mengele, who used them in his heinous human experiments at Auschwitz concentration camp. Surely Sir Cyril would have fit well into that environment.

Burt went on to be the principal architect of the infamous 11+ examination, where children were more likely to be accepted for grammar school if they were from middle-class families. Even then, in some parts of the country, as few as three percent of those taking the 11+ test qualified for a grammar school education. And no need to imagine how Burt's prejudices influenced the test: detailed analysis of the 11+ system showed a strong class bias in the examination. For example, questions about the role of household servants or classical composers were far easier for middle-class children to answer than those from less wealthy, less educated backgrounds. True enough: for the longest time I thought Mo Zart was a German soccer player!

But one man does not an educational system make. Where were all the decent, fair-minded, unprejudiced, British educators and law-makers of the day? Where indeed?

As one of those "lower class" individuals who came close to being excluded from a grammar school education, I take great satisfaction in noting that while Cyril Burt graduated with a Second Class Honors degree, I graduated with a First Class Honors degree. And went on to gain my doctorate in the laboratories of a Nobel prize-winning laureate.

Somehow, I think that Burt would have remained unconvinced.

School Daze

PostScript

"Corporal Punishment reporting for duty, Sir."

"So you're Corporal Punishment, eh."

"Sir!"

"Don't answer back when you're addressing an officer."

"Should I answer forward, Sir?"

"What?"

"If I can't answer back, should I answer forward? Sir."

"You're a pain in the ass."

"Yes, Sir. But that's my job."

"What is?"

"To be a pain in the ass. Literally. That's where instruments of punishment meet the flesh. Sir."

"You're one smart-ass bastard, Corporal Punishment."

"But Sir, after the pain, the ass is supposed to smart."

"And that's why your services are no longer required. You're being demoted."

"You mean, I'll be Private Punishment, Sir? Will I be relocated to one of those 'special' dungeons?"

"As a permanent inmate, if I have my way."

"Wouldn't that be Cruel and Unusual Punishment, Sir?"

"I hope so. You've inflicted that on everyone else for far too long. You're dismissed."

"Sir, if you dismiss me, you'll miss me."

"Bugger off, Private. You'll never be missed."

"Beg to differ, Sir. Sooner or later, they'll want me back."

Corporal Punishment in British schools was finally outlawed in 1986. Too late for me; I'd have been fifty-four at the time. Sadly, the Corporal may be right: there are organizations that are actively seeking a return to those dark, dark days.

While most US states have banned corporal punishment in state schools, it continues to flourish in the Southern and Western regions of the country.

7

Rash 'n' Ing
PreScript

"I didn't read children's books when I was a child.
The only books in our house were ration books."

Michael Foreman
British Author/Illustrator
Children's Books

Right on, Mike. At our place too.
Except for a Horse Racing Guide.

Rash 'n' Ing
Script

Soon after war was declared, Germany began its attempt to starve the UK into submission by attacking merchant ships bringing food and supplies into Britain. At that time, fifty-million people depended on the importation of about seventy percent of its basic needs.

A few months later, rationing was announced. We discussed it that evening. "Yes," my father said, "We're going to have rationing." He looked at me and asked, "Do you know what that is?" he asked me.

"I think so, but what's an ing?" I asked.

"Mm?"

"What's an ing?" I repeated.

"What do you mean?"

"Well, you said we're gonna 'ave a rash and an ing. I 'ad a rash once, but I've never 'ad an ing."

My father explained.

Well, I was just seven.

For the record, I was a little ahead of my time. The Dutch company, ING, was founded in 1991, and went on to become the world's largest banking/financial services corporation.

Now *that's* an ING!

Gasoline was the first commodity to be controlled; dairy products, meat, and sugar quickly followed. Apart from fish, vegetables, fruit, and bread, almost all other foods were added to the list. Clothes too. Eventually, whatever was not rationed proved to be of limited availability. On many an occasion, unavailable. It didn't take long for me to realize how many basic foods, like milk, I'd taken for granted.

As we discussed the list, my father paused after sugar, and added with, I thought, viciously insensitive cruelty, "That'll mean little or no ice cream or sweets."

That got my attention. I could do with less meat, and no vegetables was no hardship at all. In fact, that would be consistent with my preferred diet. But no ice cream? And no sweets? The reality of war was beginning to crowd in on me. "No sweets?" I repeated in disbelief. This is serious. Bloody serious.

"'ow long will this rationing last?" I asked, giving the operative word all the contempt I could muster.

"We don't know. For the duration of the war, probably."

"More than a week?"

"Oh yes. I'm sure of that."

"More than two weeks?"

They never did answer me.

Restaurants were initially exempt from rationing, but since the wealthy could afford to eat out frequently there was a public outcry. Accordingly, the cost of a meal was limited to five shillings. About a dollar at the time. A sandwich? Fish and chips?

On hearing this, I had an idea: "Why don't we eat ice cream and sweets in a restaurant? We could do that for less than five shillings."

They never did answer that question either. And anyway, I had no idea what five shillings would buy. That was way above my pay grade, as they say.

The government encouraged us to grow our own vegetables. Lawns and flowers were ripped up to produce something to eat. The national campaign was "Dig for Victory." So we dug. We had at most fifty square feet of questionably usable soil in our back yard, and we optimistically planted a variety of new seeds. Within months we harvested...old seeds. I now wonder if, technically, the results of our "Dig for Defeat" constituted treason? In any event, for many of us city people, it all came down to:

Give me Rations, or Give me Death.

Inevitably, a black market quickly thrived, and a type of petty criminal who dealt in illicit goods of all kinds, including rationed food and clothing, emerged. The spiv. He was typically a hustling, streetwise, gaudily dressed cockney, and regarded as something of a lovable rogue. Nevertheless, well over 100,000 prosecutions took place.

Our immediate neighborhood could boast at least two violators. I confess to my own black market involvement elsewhere. The other incident involved one of our neighbors. She was fined for using four ration books to buy food for her family of three. Her fifteen-year-old son had accidentally been sent both a child's book and an adult's book and, for many months, she had illegally obtained extra supplies. She claimed she thought the extra rations were because her son was a particularly big boy. Thank goodness they didn't allocate according to size. On that basis, I might have been given half-rations.

Lest you think that the enviably civilized Brits were above other war-related crimes, they weren't. Looting, during and after an air raid, was quite common. The blackout proved to be the pickpocket's good friend, and molesters of women had a field day—or should I say field night. 'Cause that, they said, was when the "naughty stuff" took place. I never did know what they meant by naughty stuff.

Government scams were common. A friend of the family loved to tell us about his neighbor, Walter Handy, who took more than full advantage of the government's program that paid five hundred pounds to those who'd lost their homes to bomb damage. Mr. Handy claimed to have been "bombed out" nineteen times in a five-month period. He was jailed for three years. Prostitution flourished. Murder victims were sometimes hidden among the rubble resulting from an air raid, where they might be assumed to be casualties of a bombing raid. I wonder if perps thought that a bullet in the forehead, or death by strangulation, could be blamed on the Germans. Then again, why not! They were bastards anyway!

A wartime crime rate increase of 57% was a tolerable level of civilian lawlessness. But, dear reader, note that my own undiscovered crime, that I promise to tell you about shortly, wasn't included in the statistics. That could nudge it up a tad.

So there were hardships, but with the Londoner's usual blend of cockiness and defiance, we survived. Unexpectedly, rationing actually improved the health of the British people. Infant mortality declined, and life expectancy rose as people still had access to enough of a varied diet.

Hard to believe that being on the receiving end of the Battle of Britain could actually result in a rise in life expectancy. The more than 40,000 poor sods who died in the Blitz might want to argue that.

In late 1940, I was nearly eight years old. London had already endured relentless German bombing, and the results were everywhere to be seen. Harry Felton and I were bike buddies. We'd ride around the streets, checking out the new terrain that the German bombers had thoughtfully created. Many streets were closed off or reconfigured, and new, rubble-strewn alleyways emerged. The leveling of houses and buildings allowed us to see more of our surroundings than was previously available to us. While we often found ourselves in unfamiliar streets, it was always a mission-accomplished end to the adventure when we found our way home. Neither Harry nor I could claim to have a good sense of direction, but we got to the other end when we had to, and learned something about perseverance in the process.

It was a bright, sunny day when we discovered an area we'd never seen before. At the end of a "new" cul-de-sac, we came across what seemed to be a large patch of ground covered in wild flowers. A rare sight indeed, since the "Dig for Victory" campaign had led most people to sacrifice the visuals for the edibles.

Flowers were good for the soul, but not for the belly.

The colorful display we were looking at wasn't enclosed. There was no fence. No wall. No sign, and no one around. It seemed so inviting. We gathered a few of those blooming beauties—just whatever would fit in one small hand; we still had to ride our bikes home. I was eager to present my trophy to my mother who was unwell at the time. They'd cheer her up, I thought.

We'd left our bikes behind a nearby bush. As we were walking back to them, a large, angry-looking, old man suddenly appeared behind us, yelling "'Ere you two. What the...."

We'd heard enough. We dropped the flowers that seemed to wilt before they hit the ground, and turned to run. Harry was on my right, away from Mr. Big-and-Scary, and my nimble friend ran like hell. An ugly, earth-encrusted hand grabbed the back of my collar and literally lifted me up clear off the ground.

"You're comin' with me," he snarled. "I'm gonna 'and you over to the police."

I was scared. Scared to death. Air raids, bombs, anti-aircraft guns, flaming airplanes crashing to the ground, emergency vehicles, and the screams of people in anticipation of death or in the throes of it, were and will always be memorably vivid. But none of these could compare with the fear I had, not of being arrested, but of confronting my mother over the incident.

Mr. Big half dragged me out into the nearby Mile End Road, and towards the police station that was a few hundred feet further on. He was cursing, swearing, threatening me with all kinds of punishment. He seemed to feed on his own rage, becoming more incensed with every stride. As my own fear grew, so I instinctively tried to hold back a little. To slow him down, if I could, even if, in the process, his grip did pull my collar tighter around my neck. My tactic obviously angered him. Swinging his free, outstretched arm, he slapped the side of my head with his open hand. Hard. I remember screaming with a particularly loud "owww" in response. At that very moment, and quite by chance, a London bobby (policeman) was walking towards us, presumably having just left the police station. Just as the constable reached us, Mr. Big pulled me to a stop, and blurted out, "I caught 'im stealin' me flowers, and I'm taking 'im to the station." The bobby looked at him, then at me, and then again at Mr. Big, and said, "Okay, but be sure to tell the sergeant that you hit him." Mr. Big scowled, mumbled something, and continued dragging me ever closer to the familiar Blue Lamp bearing the words "Police Station" that hung over the entranceway. I'd never been inside one of these places before, and I certainly wasn't looking forward to my first visit. With less than twenty feet to go, Mr. Big abruptly stopped, pulled me up by my collar, shook me hard, and said something about letting me off with a warning this time, but if I did it again...

As soon as I felt his grip relax, I pulled away, and ran as fast as I could, faster than I'd ever run before. Back to my bike. Back home. Back to my unknowing mother.

"Did you have a nice bike ride, dear?" she asked.

"Yeah. It was fun." *Sort of.*

Ever since that experience, any time I present flowers I'd bought for someone, I think of those wild flowers that never made it to my mother's vase. I still believe that freshly picked wild flowers have a special quality that a florist's offering can never match. The immortal words of the English poet, Rupert Brooke, come to mind:

> "Unkempt about those hedges blows
> An English unofficial rose."

I was grateful to the policeman who intervened. In that era, the London bobby carried a silver whistle, and a short, wooden truncheon. No other weapons or devices. No guns. No handcuffs. No tasers, No nonsense. They were the friends of the law-abiding. Friends of the victims. And respected by all, including the bad guys.

Those were the days, my friend.
We thought they'd never end.

Sadly, they did.

Rash 'n' Ing
PostScript

The Second World War ended in 1945, yet food rationing in the UK continued until 1954, another nine years. Bread, which was never rationed during wartime, was put "on the ration" in July, 1946. It wasn't until the early 1950s that most commodities were finally de-rationed.

Why so late? Since much of Britain's food was imported, the simple answer was that there was too little foreign currency available to pay for it. {Shame we couldn't settle the debt with confiscated Deutschmark). In fact, the country had been flirting with bankruptcy for years. Much of the economy had been directed to wartime needs, and the readjustment to a peacetime economy was a slow and difficult process. By the end of the war, British exports were at a fraction of its prewar level. The UK had been sustained by the US Lend-Lease program, but only for the duration of the war. In 1945, it was time to pay the piper. So we repaid our multibillion-dollar debt to the US. Slowly, however. Very slowly. America had provided a loan equivalent to $56 billion (in 2013 dollars) that was supposed to tide the Brits over until they got back on their feet. British politicians had been hoping for a gift, but that was not to be. It took time to repay the US loan; the last payment was made in 2006. Win or lose, the cost of war is brutal. In people, property, and cold, hard cash.

Food rationing began in January, 1940, when importing food into Britain quickly became difficult and dangerous: German U-boats did their best to prevent supplies from reaching us. The different categories of food were progressively added to the list of rationed goods. Sadly, and misguidedly, homegrown vegetables were not rationed. Damn!

From my pseudo-urchin perspective, one of the more sensible restrictions was that of soap: it stayed in limited supply until late 1950. Personally, I was all in favor of keeping it in a perpetual state of restricted access. Sugar, on the other hand, was one of the very last things to be de-rationed. Not until late 1953. As a chocoholic, I took this very much to heart—and stomach. Thirteen years of irreplaceably lost indulgences. Sometimes I think I'm still trying to sate the insatiable.

And how did I fare personally? Well, I was twenty-one in 1954 when rash 'n' ing for me was finally over. I was then old enough and able enough to buy all the candy

I wanted. And I tried. But somehow it was all too late. I'd missed the moment. Thereafter, I always felt that the bloody Nazis owed me six years' worth of candy indulgence. Unfortunately, there are some debts that cannot be paid.

And what was the story in the US? Much more civilized. After three years, rationing came to an end in 1946.

So I made a big mistake. I didn't leave London for America until 1959. I should have emigrated in 1946, while there was still time for me to make up the sugar deficit. On the other hand, the delay may have saved me a few teeth.

8

Gas, Gas Masks, and Gasoline
PreScript

UK scientists had developed the "M Device," an exploding shell containing the highly toxic gas, diphenylaminechloroarsine. It was described as "The most effective chemical weapon ever devised." Uncontrollable vomiting, coughing up blood, and instant, crippling fatigue were the most common reactions.

They remind me of how I reacted to my first wife's stipulations for my divorce: my castration was at the top of her list.

But seriously folks, when the M Device was presented to Churchill's cabinet members, they were hostile to the use of such weapons—much to his irritation. "I am strongly in favour of using poisoned gas," he declared in a secret memorandum, and criticized his colleagues for their "squeamishness."

Churchill was relentless. "If the bombardment of London became a serious nuisance…I should be prepared to do anything that would hit the enemy…I may certainly have to ask you to support me in using poison gas. We could drench…cities in Germany in such a way that most of the population would be requiring constant medical attention. We could stop all work at the flying bomb starting points. I do not see why we should have the disadvantages of being the gentleman while they have all the advantages of being the cad. There are times when this may be so but not now…

…I shall ask you to drench Germany with poison gas, and if we do it, let us do it one hundred per cent. In the meanwhile, I want the matter studied in cold blood by sensible people and not by that particular set of psalm-singing uniformed defeatists which one runs across now here now there…I shall of course have to square Uncle Joe (Stalin) and the President (Roosevelt); but you need not bring this into your calculations at the present time. Just try to find out what it is like on its merits."

In other words, "If we're gonna git 'em, let's git 'em!" More power to Winnie. The man had balls!

Perhaps discouraged by the other side's ability to retaliate, neither the UK nor Nazi Germany ever used poison gases during World War II.

Gas, Gas Masks, and Gasoline
Script

The British government issued gas masks to everyone in the UK. By 1940, thirty-eight million masks had been circulated. We were instructed to carry them everywhere. Adults typically found them to be unpleasant to use: they were uncomfortable, and they smelled of rubber. My friends and I, or, as I would have said at the time, "me 'n' me mates," thought they were great. We put them on and, pretending we were monsters from outer space, scared little kids—littler than we were anyway. We could also pass for the weirdo who lived at Number 47; he'd have been on a sexual predator list if we'd have had one at the time. Our pièce de résistance, however, was that we could force air out of the mask, and produce disgusting noises.

Needless to say—a stupid phrase! If it's needless to say, why am I saying it? Oh well, I've come this far, so...needless to say, many of us were quite capable of producing disgusting noises without gas masks.

We participated in gas attack drills, but never had to use our masks in response to an actual enemy attack. We were lucky. There could have been problems. I have to wonder how well those masks of yesteryear might have functioned when put to the test. In particular, I wonder about their effectiveness in the presence of phosgene, Germany's preferred choice of poisonous gas in World War I.

Soon after the war began, broad rationing of food was imposed. What wasn't rationed, was often scarce with sharp increases in prices. I think I mentioned earlier that people could eat reasonably well in restaurants. This, of course, favored the wealthy who could afford to dine out. Such was privilege, even in the time of war. Especially in the time of war!

The first commodity to be rationed was gasoline; its availability for personal use was strictly limited, and it remained rationed until five years after the end of the war. Personal use gasoline was colorless. Fuel supplied to "approved users," typically those involved in war-related or commercial activities, was dyed red. Its use for nonessential purposes was a punishable offense.

And that takes us back to the WWII gas mask. In addition to a fiber filter, its canister also contained granules of activated charcoal intended to adsorb toxic gases. You'll remember that I was given a chemistry set for my seventh birthday. So, as a budding chemist, I could scarcely resist removing the canister from a spare gas mask, and experimenting with the charcoal in a few experiments I'd read about. One, I vividly remember, was to use the charcoal to remove the color from brown sugar, rendering it white. I was fascinated by the process. But alas, the enchantment of decolorization was to lead me into the dark world of the wartime black market. Although I was but a kid at the time, as an EastEnder I was no stranger to brushes with the law. So I brushed.

Mr. Montgomery, a neighbor of ours, owned a substantial car rental business. He had a fleet of mid-1930s vintage Daimler automobiles: elegant, black, chauffeur-driven limousines. His primary business was weddings and funerals—not his own. Others. Soon after the bombing of London began, the funeral side of his activities was in great demand. Easy to understand why. And as one of the approved users, he had ready access to dyed petrol.

I was hanging around his garage one day, when he said to me, "So, young man, I hear you're a chemist now."

I mentioned one or two of my early experiments, like turning wine into water and water back into wine. He nodded patiently. When I went on to describe my brown sugar triumphs, his interest really picked up.

"Well," he said, "if you can do that then maybe you can take the colour out of this?" He presented me with a small can of restricted-use, dyed gasoline. With a sneer that was the closest he could get to a smile, he added, "I'll make it worth your while." I didn't know what my while was worth, but I thought I'd defer to his generosity—if I was successful. I also felt it necessary to defer to him personally. Mr. Montgomery was a large, mostly bald man with a gruff, somewhat threatening personality. Intimidating. So I yielded to the promise of a reward for success, behind which lurked the potential for incurring his displeasure for failure. I focused more on the stick than I did on the carrot.

I took his can of gas back to my laboratory—a small wooden box in the corner of my tiny bedroom—and got to work. With access to another gas mask canister, I removed the charcoal and added a handful of it to the can of gasoline. I shook the can, left it to stand for a while, and filtered the contents through more charcoal. Voilà, the fuel was clear—totally devoid of any color. With much pride, I presented it to Mr. Montgomery, and described the method I'd used. He was obviously pleased with my achievement, and promptly gave me half-a-crown; at that time that was worth about a dollar in buying power. I subsequently learned that he was a frequent participant in black market activities, so I can only guess what he did with my methodology. I didn't know anything about the black market, but I did know a veritable fortune when I saw one. And a half-a-crown was one. Sadly, no one told me about royalties. Mr. Montgomery certainly didn't.

Those war years forced a young boy to grow up fast, especially in a working-class environment, where young kids were exposed to all kinds of hardships, influences, temptations, threats, and dangers. Playing in the streets with older boys inevitably helped us develop street smarts, survivor skills, and instincts. It was rather like being exposed to and surviving infectious organisms—what didn't kill us made us stronger.

By the way, I didn't tell my mother about my little "consulting" venture; intuitively, I knew she wouldn't have approved. So not a word, please.

Gas, Gas Masks, and Gasoline
PostScript

In those early WWII years, we participated in gas attack drills, using our masks. But only for short periods of time. Fortunately. We've now recognized that the filters in the issued gas masks contained respirable asbestos fibers. Breathing in asbestos fibers can lead to protracted deaths from diseases like lung cancer and mesothelioma. In other words, we could have killed ourselves...slowly. Slowly, but surely.

Out of ignorance, callous indifference, or greed, and despite our current awareness of the asbestos hazards of those old masks, and their illegality, they're still being sold on eBay. I just checked. A few bucks will get you a mask—and, if you wear or handle it very much, a good possibility of a lingering death.

By chance, just a couple of years after the war, I was working in the laboratories of a small pharmaceutical company, the British Drug Houses. Unadvisedly to be sure, I had insisted on leaving school early, and was just fifteen when I started my first full-time job. At three pounds (about seven dollars) for a forty-hour week, by the way.

I was using phosgene, formula $COCl_2$, or "Cockle-2" as we in the Chem Biz called it, in the synthesis of a series of chemical compounds known as isocyanates. I mention that only because I'm sure you'd want to know what exactly I was doing with the phosgene. I don't want you to think that I was out there trying to poison anyone. Like Mr. Montgomery, perhaps?

Knowing the hazardous properties of phosgene, I was working in a walk-in fume cupboard, wearing the best commercial gas mask available. However, the fume cupboard was old, and probably inefficiently ventilated. In a short time, the canister containing the activated charcoal that was intended to adsorb any trace amounts of phosgene in the area was quickly saturated. As soon as I detected the fresh mown hay aroma of phosgene inside the mask, even as a lowly lab assistant, I knew enough to get the hell out of there. Out of the fume cupboard, and out of the mask. In essence, what the Germans failed to do during the war, I did for them: I'd poisoned myself with deadly phosgene gas.

At that time, safety was obviously low down on the list of management concerns; in any event, there was no effective treatment for phosgene poisoning. The company nurse sent me home to spend two or three days in a quiet, darkened room. Fortunately, I didn't develop any lasting effects from the phosgene that I may have inhaled.

As I write this, I'm forced to wonder whether the lingering death I had apparently escaped has taken the form of a compulsion to write about it.

9

We're Going to America. Aren't We?
PreScript

"Enemy submarines are to be called U-Boats. The term submarine is to be reserved for Allied underwater vessels. U-Boats are those dastardly villains who sink our ships, while submarines are those gallant and noble craft which sink theirs."

Winston Churchill
Prime Minister, UK

Churchill always did choose his words carefully.

We're Going to America. Aren't We?
Script

The British strategic plan for World War II allowed for the possible deaths of up to four million civilians as victims of German aerial bombardment. Accordingly, before the Second World War began, the government had developed plans for evacuation on a massive scale. Two days before war was declared, more than a million citizens, mostly children, traveled by train, leaving cities and towns for safe areas in the countryside; there, they were assigned to live in foster homes. It wasn't surprising that not all parents embraced the scheme: their children would be taken from them, mothers wouldn't know exactly where their children were going, with whom they'd be living, or when they'd be returning home. Inevitably, there were problems. Lots of problems. Nevertheless, within a few weeks, nearly three million children had been evacuated.

Young Billy Ashton, who lived a few houses away from me, was among those three million. He and I sometimes played together. He was a rather timid five-year-old when he was evacuated to Wales. On his arrival in Llanfairpwllgwyngyllgogerychwyrndrobwyllllantysiliogogogoch, there was a problem. No, not how to pronounce the name of the town, which is real, by the way. It means, "The Church of St. Mary by the pool with the white hazel near the fierce whirlpool by St. Tysilio's church and the red cave." A different, predictable problem. An avoidable one. The identification labels his mother used were small cardboard tags attached by string: one on his coat button, and one on his lapel. So what was predictable? Rain. The ever-present drizzle that slowly and inevitably permeates everything in the UK. The cardboard tags bearing name and address quickly became soggy and unreadable.

A little kid, wandering around a station platform in a strange place was easily "lost" among dozens of other kids. The little boy with indecipherable pieces of wet cardboard attached to him was a special challenge. An assigned adult who was trying to solve the problem took him to the local police station for help.

The big sergeant stooped down, patted Billy on the head, and boomed,

"HELLO SON. AND WHAT'S YOUR NAME?"

"Billy."

"WELL, BILLY, AND WHAT'S YOUR LAST NAME?"

"Don't know."

"WHERE ARE YOU FROM, BILLY?"

"Don't know."

A second glass of milk and a third chocolate cookie weren't enough to stem Billy's tears.

Since he was with a group of children from London, the station sergeant, in a flash of Sherlockian insight, decided he was "Billy from London," adding, "Well, that narrows it down a bit."

It was days before they managed to fully identify Billy, place him with his new foster parents, and to reassure his London mother that he was alive and safe.

Some time later, I found myself to be one of those transported kids. Like so many others, I was wrapped up, tagged, and sent out to a place unknown. I finally understood what it felt like to be packaged, labeled, and shipped out by UPS. Except nobody was tracking my journey, and there was no official receipt on my arrival. But at least my ID tags were protected from the rain.

In addition to the domestic evacuation program, the British government began to view countries outside of the UK to be safer havens, not only from German bombers, but also from an increasingly probable German invasion. The plan was to send a million children to British Commonwealth countries like Canada, Australia, New Zealand, and South Africa. Many were also slated for the United States.

The question of sending British children abroad was initially rejected on the grounds of creating panic and spreading defeatism. Instead, the government decided that evacuation to rural areas of Britain should be adequate.

Adequate for the British government, perhaps, but not for the affluent, upper classes.

At the beginning of the war, America was neutral and had strict immigration laws. This presented a serious obstacle for the US to accept any significant numbers of British refugees. At the time, however, there was a private undertaking that this wasn't a British government-sponsored evacuation. Despite the political complexities, over 5,000 children landed on US soil.

Prior to the advent of a government program, evacuation to overseas countries was done privately, when children were mostly from the upper classes of society. Since the wealthier classes disproportionately populated positions of power and influence, their abandonment of the safety of underprivileged children was deeply resented. To their credit, however, and I say this as an anti-royalist, Britain's royal family elected to stay home for the duration of the war. Not to be cynical, but let's face it: there's a lot of German blood in the British royal family. Perhaps they enjoyed some kind of wartime immunity.

But I digress.

Many wanted similar evacuation options for their children, even though they were too poor to pay for the "seavacuations." In response to intense public pressure, a program was instituted where the British government would meet the cost of transportation overseas, with contributions from parents according to their ability to pay. Children selected for the program were prioritized. More than seventy years later, it's apparently still not known on what basis this was done. At the time, since selections were clearly not made on a first come, first served basis, charges soon appeared in the press that the upper classes were given priority.

Meanwhile, after their children were safely ensconced in other, safer countries, many wealthy Londoners, parents and otherwise, abandoned their London homes for the relative safety of more remote parts of the country. Expensive private hotels flourished, proving to be very popular with those gutless bastards who could afford to stay there. Hard to believe, isn't it? Even in war, privilege determined life or death!

Simmer down, old man, this is supposed to be the lighter side of London's Bloody Blitz. Remember?

By the end of 1941, parents with means or connections, were able to evacuate about 13,000 children. Three thousand were shipped, literally, to the US. For some, having relatives in America was a critical factor. And that was to be the key component of our family's plan.

My mother's sister Ann, lived in New York, having married an American many years earlier. At the time, I assumed that "New York" meant New York City. It was much later that I learned there was also a state called New York.

Thus, my brother Sidney and I were being readied to go join Aunt Ann in New York. Whichever New York that was. Sid was seven years older than I was. A chronic asthmatic, who struggled all his life with acute breathing problems. There were no effective drugs back in the 1940s, and the infamous pea-soupers of London, those dense, yellow, soot-filled fogs that were so appealingly mysterious in old movies, surely didn't help any kind of respiratory malfunction. He was charged by my parents to look after me, yet it was always clear that, despite the age difference, I would be looking after him. And a clean air, sea voyage would surely rejuvenate his severely compromised lungs.

[A parenthetic note of personal sadness: my brother made it through the war, but died at the young age of forty-seven, during one of his frequent hospital stays for acute asthmatic crisis. He breathed mostly London air during his lifetime, and crazy though it sounds now, smoked far too many cigarettes.]

And so, our small suitcases were packed; our gas masks were standing by; and a variety of identification labels awaited attachment to suitcase, gas mask box, and person. Some were even sewn inside our outer clothes.

We were ready. Well, *we* were ready!

I was very excited about America: land of cowboys and Coca-Cola, chewing gum, and drive-in movies. And yeah, a big boat ride to get there. Who knows, perhaps I'd be able to visit my father's cousin; he lived in Chicago and could show me all the gangsters I'd seen in the movies. Some of them, anyway.

What could possibly go wrong?

Well, lots, really.

We were all signed up, but had to wait for a ship assignment and departure date. Then we heard: we were scheduled to be on the British passenger ship, the *SS City of Benares*, leaving Liverpool on September 13, 1940. Destination: Canada. From there, we'd be escorted down to New York. Then we heard again: we were *not* scheduled. Not this time. Perhaps next time. The number of potential evacuees was far in excess of the available spaces. For whatever reason, there was no room for us.

I think I might guess why.

By then, U-boats were prowling the waters around the British Isles, especially to prevent the arrival of food and armaments; sinking ships leaving the UK was apparently also on their to-do list.

The Dutch liner *SS Volendam*, carrying 320 British children was torpedoed on August 30, 1940. Fortunately, all the children were saved.

The *SS City of Benares* left Liverpool, as scheduled, on September 13, 1940, with ninety children aboard. My brother and I were not among them.

Four days later, the German submarine U-48 fired two torpedoes into the *City of Benares*. Tragically, seventy-seven of the ninety children on board died at sea.

With too few escort ships available to protect evacuations by sea, Winston Churchill, the then British Prime Minister, immediately suspended all further evacuations of children to overseas locations.

And so, my brother and I were forced to remain as landlubbers. No Coca-Cola, Wrigley's gum, cowboys, and drive-ins. No big boat ride. No New York. No Chicago.

When I was told that we wouldn't be going to America because of the danger of enemy submarines, I had a great idea: I was really good at the game, "Battleships and Cruisers," even better than my older brother. Especially at sinking submarines. So I wondered: "If I can find a way to sink all the U-boats, couldn't we then go to America?" But I was forced to give up the idea: I couldn't decide how to destroy the submarines.

Couldn't sink 'em, I thought. *They're already sunk*!

When I grudgingly accepted the fact that I wasn't bound for the excitement of America, my next thought was to join "me mate," Mikey Mulligan, in Cornwall. But no. For whatever reason, I was scheduled to be evacuated to Guildford in Surrey. I had friends who had been evacuated to Scotland and found that they couldn't communicate with the locals. I knew that Guildford was only thirty miles from

London, but I did wonder whether they spoke English there—at least, my version of the language.

No, they didn't.

We're Going to America. Aren't We? PostScript

After the war, the captain of submarine U-48, Kapitan-leutnant Heinrich Bleichrodt, was charged by the Allies of war crimes related to the sinking of the *City of Benares*. Bleichrodt was accused of sinking the ship with the full knowledge that it was transporting evacuees. He denied that there was any way for him to know who was on board. He defended his attack, insisting that the British government was to blame for allowing children to travel by sea in a war zone. Not much different from blaming an attractive woman for being raped, because she was attractive. Bleichrodt was duly acquitted.

Despite the fact that Bleichrodt's crew expressed shock and regret that many children had died at the hands of U-48, Bleichrodt himself refused to apologize to the surviving families of the children lost at sea.

On behalf of the families of those seventy-seven children who drowned in the cold, rough waters of the Atlantic Ocean, I was eager to read of a just ending to the life of Heinrich Bleichrodt. Was he tried, found guilty, and put to death by some justice-seeking, anti-Nazi German organization? Was he struck down by an angry god seeking revenge and retribution?

Nah. Life doesn't work like that. Neither does death. Good old Heinrich died peacefully at the reasonable age of sixty-eight. In Germany. His fatherland. At home. In his bed. Surrounded by the many medals bestowed upon him by Adolph Hitler.

Rot in hell, Heinrich Bleichrodt! Wait a minute. I'm an atheist. There is no hell. Or heaven. Oh well, just rot!! Yes, you will, anyway, won't you. Nature takes care of that. None of this feels right. Not enough justice. Needs something more... *like Hell!*

10

The Dream Girls: Thelma and Agnes PreScript

According to experts, common sexual behaviors in school-aged children, 7-12 years, are:

- Purposefully touching private parts (masturbation), usually in private
- Playing games with children their own age that involve sexual behavior (such as "truth or dare," "playing family," or "boyfriend/girlfriend")
- Attempting to see other people naked or undressing
- Looking at pictures of naked or partially naked people
- Viewing/listening to sexual content in media (television, movies, games, music, etc.)
- Wanting more privacy (for example, not wanting to undress in front of other people) and being reluctant to talk to adults about sexual issues
- Beginnings of sexual attraction to/interest in peers

Yeah, well, maybe the experts knew all that, but no one told me. How was I to know how I should respond to the Guildford girls: to the beauty of Thelma Hodges, or to the aggressive advances of Agnes?

I escaped the ravages of wartime London only to find myself confronting love, sex, sadism, gang life, and organized crime in the civilized respectability of Guildford. In the gentle charm of the County of Surrey. Who'd've guessed?

The Dream Girls: Thelma and Agnes Script

Soon after WWII was declared, millions of Londoners, especially children, left the city for the relative safety of the British countryside. For whatever reason, we didn't leave then; my parents decided to wait a while. Nevertheless, since we were apparently determined not to miss any of the Blitz action, the first year of the war was the time to be away. And so we were. It was nearly a year before the Luftwaffe appeared over London; we had plenty of time to get back home and avoid missing a single bomb. We were loyal prey.

I don't know why or how Guildford was selected. Probably assigned by the government. But in retrospect, it wasn't the best choice. Dumb, really. Guildford was only about thirty miles outside of London—not nearly far enough away to be safe. More significantly, Guildford was southeast of London. Any German bombers that may have been chased out of London would return to the continent. France, probably. Reluctant to take undelivered bombs back with them, they'd dump them on their way home. Somewhere. Somewhere like Guildford. But all that proved to be academic, at least during our stay in that delightful little town of Guildford, in that delightful little county of Surrey. It remained delightful the whole time we were there.

My mother and I duly arrived in Guildford, and made our way to Portsmouth Road. Officials directed us to our assigned billet. Number 26. At that time, Guildford had a population of about 75,000, most of whom lived in town. Portsmouth Road ran along the outskirts of town.

Contrary to our expectations, Number 26 was no dreary little row home that many of our London neighbors had experienced in their evacuation destinations. A high stone wall guarded the estate from the riffraff.

Ironically, we were the riffraff.

The path leading to the front door was long, winding, and covered by a spectacular canopy of flowers Our new home was big. Bloody big. A veritable mansion. One that would have been ideal as a setting for a television series featuring British aristocracy. I described it, at the time, as "A bloody great 'ouse wiv 'undreds of rooms, surrounded by 'undreds of square miles of green." As I was saying, it was big!

A stone-faced butler opened the enormous front door; close behind him was the mistress of the house, Mrs.

Zillah Brake. She smiled, and said, warmly, "Welcome to Rookwood."

"Rookwood?" I repeated in obvious surprise. "Ain't we in Guildford?" Clearly, I had limited experience of houses that were significant enough to be given their own names. The only other one I knew, which was, I thought, a little less imposing, was called Buckingham Palace. One difference between the two was that I'd never been invited into the palace, while I had now not only been invited into Rookwood, but was going to live there for the foreseeable future. I made a mental note to squeeze in a visit to the king and queen later. If I had time.

Leaning on her walking stick, the frail, white-haired, and strikingly elegant Mrs. Brake told us that, together with Mrs. Gibson and her adult daughter, we'd have our own rooms near the servants' quarters. Her staff would take good care of us. And they did: the butler, the cook, the footmen, and the maids. The gardeners were always ready to chat, and even Mrs. Brake's daughter looked in on us once in a while. Mr. Brake, Squire of the Manor, had died earlier. It wasn't hard to imagine that he'd exhausted himself whipping peasants and raping local virgins. I'm not absolutely sure about that, but the good old days were, well, the good old days, so who knows?

I found it difficult to absorb the size and splendor of my new home. Though the enormous rooms with their high ceilings, stone floors, and heavy, dark, wooden paneling everywhere were cold and depressingly gloomy, I thought

I could get used to it all. Roaring log fires helped, and I took a great liking to the suits of armor seemingly at the top of every marble staircase.

On my first day at the local primary school, I fell in love. There she was, on the other side of the classroom. Thelma Hodges. About my age, long blond hair, blue eyes, and a subtle smile that Mona Lisa might envy. I had no idea how I should react to this extraordinary vision. Should I approach her? What could I say? Was it too soon to tell her that I loved her? Surely as a hip, big city kid, I should be able to charm her into submission; sweep her off her feet. Then again, I was only seven, and not too articulate. Instinctively, I knew I needed a "chick magnet," or whatever it was called in the 1940s. The only one I could think of was my developing passion for chemistry. I'd put that to work.

From something I'd never seen before, red roses growing wild in a country lane, I gathered a few petals. I placed them in an elegant perfume bottle I'd recently found, added water, and shook the suspension vigorously to extract the essence of the flower. The petals floated lazily in the bottle; it was gift-ready. But sadly, like Peanuts' Charlie Brown and his unexpressed feelings for the little red-headed girl, my love also went unspoken. We Charlie B's had much in common, even though I predated him by many years. During the whole of my Guildford stay, I never had the courage to talk to that beautiful blond vision across the room, or to present my exotic perfume to her. It was fortunate in some ways, since I later discovered that, while good to look at, my perfume was totally devoid of any aroma.

I should have known that the key ingredient in rose petal oil, beta-damascenone, which, of course, you and I know by its common name, (E)-1-(2,6,6-trimethyl-cyclohexa-1,3-dien-1-yl)but-2-en-1-one, was insoluble in water. I always blamed Mr. Pickles for not teaching me that. (You'll remember Mr. Pickles from my "School Daze," won't you?). We needed a little less ear-boxing, and a little more science. And while, according to Alfred, Lord Tennyson:

> "'Tis better to have loved and lost
> Than never to have loved at all."

Surely,

> 'Tis best to have loved and won.

The thrill of my Thelma Hodges encounter almost canceled out the downside of my Guildford school experiences. Almost—but not quite. This was to be the next level of corporal punishment. I think of it as sergeant punishment. Further, it was coupled with an unexpected measure of prejudice against Londoners. I was certainly expanding my knowledge base: I didn't know either existed.

Guilty, again, of talking in class, and, in my teacher's snarled words, "Another filthy Londoner who…." He mumbled the rest as he grabbed my wrist, held my hand palm down on my desk and, in a state of near frenzy, hit me repeatedly on the back of the hand and knuckles with a thick wooden rod.

The last thing I wanted to do was to cry. Not in front of the beautiful Miss Hodges. And I didn't cry. I sobbed. It couldn't have been worse: sobbing in front of my new classmates, and sobbing in front of the girl I loved. If ever there was a moment for an outside distraction, that was it. Where was an air raid when I needed one? Where was the shrill sound of an emergency vehicle, or another kid in the class suddenly having an apoplectic fit? Alas, there was no distraction. Only the stillness of the moment, punctuated by the whimpering of a young boy in acute physical and emotional distress. That was a feeling to be remembered. And, yes, I remember it all too vividly. And when I do, I instinctively examine the back of my left hand.

I went home for lunch that day, and my mother quickly noticed that I'd been crying. Despite my efforts to conceal it, she also saw my severely bruised and obscenely puffed up hand; it looked like it might burst open at any moment. She immediately frog-marched me back to the school, and fiery, ever-protective mother that she was, didn't hesitate to do battle with both teacher and headmaster. I tried to distance myself from that encounter, but if anyone could give 'em hell, she could. And did.

'Tis best to have fought and won!

No teacher ever hit me again in that school. I guess hitting me was her prerogative, which she exercised rarely, but always fairly and well-intentioned. And I never cried when she punished me.

When I wasn't at school, I spent hours exploring my new environment. Lush, green, rolling hills surrounded Rookwood. A nearby meadow was covered in buttercups, dazzlingly yellow in the bright sunshine. The crystal clear waters of a nearby stream gurgled and bubbled. The air was fresh and clean. No London smog. No noisy London traffic. No East End poverty. It was another world.

It was also another house. A very different house. There were so many rooms, storage areas, and stairways to explore. A perfect place, I thought, to play hide and seek; there were nooks and crannies everywhere. I even found crannies inside some of the nooks.

As I wandered around from room to room, I gradually became aware of someone following me, peering around corners, watching my every move. I was gazing at the contents of a huge, walk-in pantry, when a young girl's head finally leaned out from behind a curtain and smiled. Wearing a black uniform with white trim, she stepped into full view. I later learned that she was a scullery maid. A kind of maid in training. A big, well-developed sixteen-year-old, she had full breasts and thick, heavy legs. Her short straight black hair, fringed in front didn't exactly reek of chic, but her constant, sheepish, and rather toothy grin did convey warm and friendly.

The girl-woman towered over me. I looked up at her and said, "'Ullo." She continued to grin, but said nothing. We continued to look at each other. As if it were the climax of a magic trick, she dramatically produced a large, red apple and held it out to me.

"Ooh, fanks," I said. I loved apples, and this one was a beaut. She continued to smile, and continued to say nothing. She then scurried away.

The second day seemed to be a repeat of the first. My second apple, another juicy gem, dangled before me.

"Ta," I said. "Ta very much." I might not have had good command of the language, but I did have good manners.

As I reached up to take the once-forbidden fruit, she took my hand and, guiding it to her right breast, pressed it firmly against her nipple. I felt a slight bump. If she wanted me to check her heart, I should tell her I didn't know how to do that. The bump felt like a small button. I pushed it. Perhaps it opened something, I thought. She moved my hand up and down, to and fro, and smiled. It was a different kind of smile. Whatever was going on, was fine with me. Those apples were damn good!

The third day of our unusual relationship was different. My new friend was waiting for me in the kitchen. Grinning as usual. She held out a glass bowl full of silver foil-covered chocolates. She nodded at me. I took one, opened it, and gazed in admiration at a ball of white chocolate with a hazelnut on top. I'd never seen anything like it. I gobbled it up, as any deprived scavenger in constant search for sweet stuff would. She nodded again. I took another.

Another nod. Another chocolate. I could play this game forever, I thought.

My total preoccupation with hazelnut-topped, white chocolate balls came to a crashing halt. Quite suddenly, she reached down to Mr. Wiggly and began to push and squeeze him, gently at first, and then more vigorously.

"*'Ere, wajafink you're doin'!*" I remember crying. But as I began to pull away from her, I felt a confusing mixture of embarrassment, panic, and pleasure. Pleasure won. I liked it. I really liked it. I was transfixed, not knowing what I should do next, or more accurately, what she was going to do next. Meanwhile, she continued to squeeze Mr. Wiggly, and I continued to like it. As I said, really like it. She again took my hand and pushed it hard on her right breast, The bump was back, bigger and harder than before. It seemed fine, I decided; at least I didn't break it the previous time.

We both half-turned to face the sound of heavy footsteps on the stone floor. They were coming towards us. Without a word, and no longer grinning, she again scurried away. I remained, standing there. I could feel my face burning and my heart pounding.

The cook stepped in, and clearly agitated, snapped, "Have you seen Agnes?" I shrugged. So that was her name. The cook continued, "That girl never comes when I call her," adding, "I know she's not very bright, and can't talk, but she *can* hear me."

So that was why Agnes never said anything to me. She couldn't. At least using words. But she could say a helluva lot with her hands and bumps.

At first, I was pleasantly full. Then, quite miserable. Within an hour, I began to feel sick. My mother couldn't understand why I didn't want dinner that evening. Must have been something I ate, she decided. I never told her that it was those delicious chocolates, specially made for the family even in heavily rationed, wartime, wealth-finds-a-way Britain; they were just too rich for my out-of-practice digestive system. But it was a sacrifice I had to make.

I checked Mr. Wiggly out that night to see if he was damaged in any way. He seemed fine. I thought a lot about my encounters with Agnes, and wondered if I should tell my mother. But I didn't think she'd understand. And anyway, she'd probably want to put a stop to it, and I wasn't sure if I wanted her to. Thelma was beautiful to look at, but Agnes made me feel good and gave me apples and chocolates. I was confused. Later, it occurred to me that Thelma and Agnes did have one thing in common: neither of them had ever said a single word to me. Unfortunately, I was far too young and inexperienced to appreciate the pure joy of being with a woman who said nothing.

Now that's bloody chauvinistic, isn't it?

Nevertheless, no misunderstandings. No criticisms. No disappointments. Yes, the innocence of youth. But even at that age, I did know one thing: I could understand war much better than I could understand girls.

Over time, I saw less and less of Agnes and more and more of the cook. Mrs. Murgatroyd proved to be a force in the Brake household. A big, solidly built fifty-something, I now think of her as a prototypic Julia Child. Her dark red hair, gathered in a tight bun, promised order and control. In contrast, her fiery green eyes said "dangerous when provoked." Either way, no one messed with this complex lady whose smile could turn to anger and back again all too quickly.

One odd thing I remember about the way of life in and around the kitchen: while the rest of the staff appeared to move slowly and deliberately, almost in slow motion, Mrs. M. functioned at a frenetic pace. It was like two superimposed time warps. Yet it all seemed to work.

I was lucky. Mrs. Murgatroyd took an early shine to me. Any time I wandered into her territory she'd find something special to give me. Usually something sweet, like apple/blackberry pie. Still one of my favorites. And then an astonishing discovery: I learned that it was possible to keep ice cream frozen in one's home. I didn't realize that that was possible. Back in Bow, neither we nor most of our neighbors had a refrigerator. Rookwood had three! And when my new benefactor added a scoop of ice cream to my warm piece of pie, I decided to stay in Guildford forever. And I didn't even have to play the breast game to enjoy all the treats I received.

I'm not sure what drove me to explore other Guildfordian lifestyles—perhaps it was my way of avoiding additional woman troubles. Okay, as a seven-and-a-half-year-old, girl troubles. In any event, I instinctively sought to escape by pursuing a whole new adventure: I became a member of a local gang.

Ironically, back in rough, tough London, where rough, tough gangs were quite common, "me 'n' me mates" weren't members of any gang, we just "hung out," or whatever it was called in the nineteen forties. No leader. No initiation. No rules. But in Guildford, I'd now moved up to the big leagues.

The house next door to Rookwood was perhaps a quarter of a mile away. That's where Jeremy's headquarters were. A wooden shed midst their acres of rolling green hills and professionally manicured gardens.

In those days, a Londoner surrounded by anything green was probably in the middle of one of our dense smogs we called "pea-soupers." I had to admit, the Guildford green was a lot more pleasant. And healthier.

Jeremy's gang consisted of a handful of local kids, and one evacuee: me. I was also the youngest and smallest. The oldest and tallest was our leader, Jeremy. He was a six-foot, skinny fifteen-year-old. He told us exactly what to do and when, and financed the operation by stealing money from his mother. At meetings, we all had to smoke cigarettes that he provided. They were a leading brand called "Players." He also insisted that we inhale deeply, as he did. It must have been the inhalation, since I found his cigarettes much more of a challenge to cough through than the brown paper cigarettes we puffed on back home. There, we couldn't afford real "fags," so we rolled our own. No tobacco. Just plain brown paper. The acrid smoke irritated the back of the throat. It wasn't too cool at the front either, but we were at war, and we had to make sacrifices. It was our duty.

"Long live the King."

"Rule Britannia."

"*'itler is a git!*"

In addition to providing cigarettes, Jeremy also lavished money on us. Lots of money. Huge amounts of money. Five shillings at a clip. That's five bob. Sixty pence. About a dollar. As I was saying, a huge amount. Our loyalty obviously came at a price. We were instructed to buy something, anything, and report back. We had complete freedom to decide on how to spend the money, but we were to tell no one where it came from. The sudden influx of extraordinary wealth presented a special problem: how could I spend it without arousing the curiosity and suspicion of my eagle-eyed mother?

There was a shop in town that sold toy soldiers. One of my favorite playthings. My involvement in many a toy soldier battle between England and Germany, despite our victory after victory, was not yet done. So, since I couldn't take new, freshly painted toy soldiers back home, back to Rookwood, I deliberately aged them by roughening them on a brick wall. She'd never notice, I thought. Wrong again. She could, and she did. I quickly yielded to her vicious interrogation methods that, in retrospect, were akin to waterboarding, and confessed to all my gang activities. My mother subsequently paid a visit to Jeremy's mother, a landed gentry neighbor of the Brakes. Jeremy's mater, as he called her, said that, yes, her son was a little on the "naughty side." She'd have a chat with him. That was the extent of his punishment. Meanwhile, my brief stay in the big leagues of crime was over, and soon after, so were my wild sex orgies. Agnes had apparently lost interest.

And so we prepared to return to London, leaving Guildford more or less as we found it. I was already focusing on my return to brown paper cigarette smoking "wiv me mates," and to new battles with my old soldiers. There were no new soldiers to play with, however; they were confiscated. No way could I be allowed to profit from my venture into the world of organized crime.

The Dream Girls: Thelma and Agnes PostScript

Three years had passed since my Guildford sojourn, when we received word that Jeremy had been killed. On his eighteenth birthday. Trying out his new motorbike on a rain-slicked road. He'd skidded under a truck, beheading himself in the process.

Perhaps I was already immune to the realities of wartime death and dismemberment to be too moved by Jeremy's demise. Perhaps I didn't know him that well. Perhaps I was an insensitive, little bastard who was preoccupied with his own survival. In any event, the grieving process was brief. There was another, more profound reason for my self-absorption: sex.

On the day that I heard about Jeremy's death, my thoughts inevitably returned to Guildford, and to the women in my life. Okay, girls. That night I had my first wet dream. It was memorably vivid: Agnes and Thelma Hodges were taking turns playing with Mr. Wiggly. The following morning my pajama pants were as stiff as a board. I rolled them up, as best I could, and hid them in the bottom of the laundry basket. My mother would never notice.

Memories die hard. Erections don't.

11

The Mean McMeanies
PreScript

As reported in the St. Ives Times
August 15, 1940.

Lady Cecilia Smythe-Blenkinsop, Mayor of St. Ives, in the county of Cornwall, welcomed a large group of London evacuees with the following statement:

"On behalf of the Council of St. Ives, I hereby welcome the many children who have been evacuated from London to join us here in our beautiful and peaceful St. Ives. It will be our responsibility to care for and protect these innocent beings, until they are, once again, able to return home safely and be reunited with their families.

"I know I speak for all of us when I say that we extend to them our warmest welcome.

"*Kern a'gas Dynnergh*—Welcome to Cornwall."

Applause.

The Mean McMeanies
Script

Mikey Mulligan lived across the street; we were good friends. In frequent "stone fights," where we'd throw small stones (and sometimes not so small stones) at the "invaders" (typically kids from nearby Merchant Street who came to do battle), Mikey and I were a team. He was really good, and could throw hard and straight; I claimed to be better. On one occasion I was a bit too good: from fifty feet away, I hit a kid near his left eye. He was taken to hospital, and fortunately, for both of us, no permanent damage was done. I don't know how the other kid reacted to the experience, but I do know it scared the hell out of me. A bobby visited us later that day and read us the riot act. Mikey wasn't being magnanimous when he confessed to being the guilty stone thrower. This was a matter of street pride; we both claimed to be the perp. Even though Mikey and I could never agree on whose stone it was, we did agree, reluctantly, to end our stone fighting careers that day. The fact that our parents threatened us with vague but severe punishment had little to do with our joint decision. Well, perhaps a little….

While we may have stopped actively throwing stones, it didn't mean we'd lost interest in it. No point wasting that well-earned skill. There was much talk about the possibility of a German invasion and, all too quickly, the possibility became the probability. We'd all been told we had to be ready, and Mikey and I were. So was the secret weapon that we'd hidden away. A nearby row home that had been gutted by a bomb, and boarded up to prevent access, was the perfect spot. As adventurous young boys with time and determination, we found a way in, and used what was left of Number 28 as our hideout. It was the equivalent of a treehouse to kids with no ready access to trees. One of the upsides of bomb damage.

Our headquarters were appealingly hazardous inside: the floor between upstairs and down was largely missing, and broken floorboards and long lengths of wire and pipes hung down perilously above broken furniture, unwanted clothing, and old newspapers. It was there that we'd gathered a large pile of small stones and other throwable pieces of glass and shrapnel. We were ready for the German invaders. We weren't going down without a fight.

At that time in our young lives, evacuation was the topic of the moment. Mikey and I shared our future plans. I was going to America with my older brother; Mikey was off to St. Ives in Cornwall. He was unusually excited, and was looking forward to a great experience. An extended stay at the far western tip of England's southern coast, three-hundred miles from London, Cornwall was one of the most popular holiday resort areas in the UK. What we'd both come to learn, however, was that while there were many heartwarming stories of the care and concern of foster parents, sadly, there were some really painful experiences too. Literally. Poor cockney kids may have been struggling for survival in a brutal war, but they weren't always welcome by the rest of the country. Too many potential foster parents proved to be openly hostile to working-class kids from London. A commonly held view was that most of the inner city kids were ill-mannered bedwetters infested with head lice. Inevitably, some were, and that didn't help the EastEnders' overall image. All too often, there was cruelty to rival what we might have expected from a Nazi occupation. And wasn't home-grown cruelty somehow more repulsive?

Over time, Mikey filled in all the details for me.

The selection process for evacuees could be a shatteringly painful experience: newly arrived children were gathered together somewhere in the village, and potential hosts took their pick. To hear, "I'll take that one," was a phrase to remember, especially if you were one of the last ones selected. Pretty little girls and clean little boys went early in the process. On the day he arrived in St. Ives, rough, tough Mikey Mulligan was the very last child taken. If I know Mikey, and I did know Mikey, he probably said to himself, "*Fuck 'em!*"

You can take the boy out of London, but
You can't take London out of the boy!

Mr. and Mrs. Alex McMean, whose name, they insisted, was pronounced "McMe-an," were wealthy landowners. Their expansive house was set within one of the largest farms in the West Country. The McMeans, known locally as the McMeanies because of their unfriendly ways, made it quite clear that they didn't want any "grubby urchins from the East End" soiling their home. But their objections didn't help. Knowing they'd be fined if they refused, they obeyed the law, and Michael Mulligan became their charge. And speaking of which, the fact that they didn't need the small allowance paid to cover Mikey's food, bedding, and clothes expenses, didn't stop them from taking it.

Mikey met the McMeans briefly—just once when he first arrived. Thereafter, he received all his instructions from Joseph, the old butler. Significantly stooped by osteoarthritis, Joseph now struggled to complete his everyday chores. His severely affected spine and joints left him in chronic pain. At that time, a high dose of aspirin was, basically, the only treatment available. Unfortunately, relief, such as it was, was accompanied by frequent episodes of stomach ulcers. No, Joseph had little to feel happy about, and adding Mikey to the old man's responsibilities, was clearly an added, unwanted burden. All too frequently, Joseph would remind the young boy of that.

When Mikey wasn't at school he was forced to work on the farm, doing the most menial of jobs: cleaning out pigsties and barns, and whatever fetching and carrying tasks were necessary. He also had to pick fruit, which he wasn't allowed to eat. At the end of each day, he was usually fed only cold food, and locked in his bedroom until "released" the following morning to prepare for school.

Mikey was a tough EastEnder. A survivor. Whether allowed to or not, he ate his fill of strawberries, raspberries, and gooseberries. On several occasions, Mikey was caught eating the berries he'd picked, and was punished by receiving no dinner that night. Although they believed in corporal punishment, the McMeans didn't want to be too close to their "unclean urchin" in order to inflict it. And if they did, knowing Mikey, he'd probably threaten to touch and infect them with "East End Evil." So the butler did it!

In English mystery stories, doesn't he always?

Old Joseph, miserable sod that he was, was always ready to provide pain on behalf of the McMeans. He saw it as his duty. And, apparently his pleasure.

Mikey's experiences proved to be quite mixed. A few families had invited him into their homes for "Cornish Cream Teas." He described these as a light afternoon meal consisting of tea, scones, clotted cream, and jam. I'd never heard of a Cornish Cream Tea before, and, suffering through the many agonies of rationing, could only drool at the thought of cream with anything.

But that was the good stuff. On the other side of the ledger, Mikey had tasted discrimination: he'd been in several fights with local kids who, ganging up on him, would yell, "All you dirty Londoners should go back to where you came from!" Mikey actually thought that that was a good idea.

One of Mikey's stories, rich in exquisite irony, will always remain my favorite. Read this, and tell me what you think.

In addition to the chores he did around the farm, every Monday, Wednesday, and Friday, at exactly 6:00 p.m., Mikey had to take two large carrier bags full of sealed paper packets down to the bottom of the McMean's half-mile-long drive. There, he would give the bags and their contents to a Mr. Smith, who'd be waiting in a black Ford Anglia automobile. In return, Mr. Smith would give Mikey a sealed envelope.

All the details had been worked out months earlier. The McMeans and Mr. Smith no longer wanted to be seen together. From the beginning, old Joseph was the go-between, but he had increasing difficulties carrying heavy bags down the long driveway. And the walk back, uphill, was an even greater ordeal. And so Mikey was instructed to do the job for him. He quickly realized that the bags he was delivering contained meat, and that the envelope he received in return contained money. Even though he was well aware of rationing, since nobody told him what the McMeans and Mr. Smith were up to, he could only wonder.

At that time, Mikey had never heard of the black market, nor did he realize that he was now a cog in its ugly wheel.

On a particularly miserable, cold, rainy evening, Mikey duly half-dragged his two heavy bags to the bottom of the driveway. Under an oak tree that had long shed its leaves, he waited. And waited. At nearly six-thirty, Mr. Smith drove up, and with no apology, hurriedly took the bags from Mikey. Holding two envelopes, Mr. Smith said, "Here's one," handing Mikey the usual thick, sealed envelope." Mikey stuffed it into his pocket to keep it out of the rain. "And here's another," Mr. Smith added. "Tell Mr. McMean this one's from the Peterson Brothers. He'll understand. The second envelope was also sealed, but was somewhat thinner. Mikey quickly put that into a separate pocket, said "Bye," and ran back up the hill. Joseph was waiting impatiently.

Mikey held out the thick envelope to Joseph. The butler snatched it angrily, and snapped, "You're late!"

"But—" Mikey spluttered.

"Don't interrupt," Joseph ordered. "And you're dripping water all over the floor!" he added, slapping the back of Mikey's head with an open palm. "Ow!" Mikey cried out as he rubbed the back of his head. Slowly, and perhaps somewhat reluctantly, he put his hand in his pocket to retrieve the second envelope. Before he could withdraw it, however, a bell rang impatiently, summoning Joseph to his master. As the butler scurried away he half-turned to Mikey and said, "Clean that mess up, and get up to your room. And don't expect any supper tonight."

Mikey hesitated for a few moments, wondering if he shouldn't just keep the Peterson contribution, whatever it was, as retaliation. But he resisted the temptation. Reluctantly, he placed the second envelope on the side table where several letters were waiting to be mailed. Among them was a large, unsealed envelope containing two of his school essays, a few clips from local newspapers, and Mikey's weekly letter home. Joseph had warned him to write good things; no complaints. He knew that they censored his letters, but he also knew that his mother liked to receive his weekly envelope, regardless of what was in it.

The next morning, and quite unbeknownst to Mikey, Joseph picked up the boy's large envelope, emptied out the contents, read his letter, and hastily pushed everything back into the envelope. Inadvertently, Joseph gathered up the second envelope that Mr. Smith had given Mikey on the previous evening, and included that.

Several days later, Mikey's mother was quite shocked when she opened Mikey's envelope and the sealed envelope within it. She slowly picked up and stared at a wad of large, white, very thin, five-pound notes. She counted them. And counted them again. All fifty of them. She couldn't believe her eyes. Two-hundred-and-fifty pounds? That was almost a year's wages for Mikey's father. "Cor blimey," she finally whispered.

Long distance telephone calls in the lives of EastEnders were both rare and expensive. So when Mikey's mother telephoned, he knew it was a rare and expensive necessity.

"It's for you," Joseph snarled, holding the phone out to Mikey. "And I'll be listening," he added, menacingly.

And in typical cockney dialect, here's their conversation, or should I say, 'ere's their conversation:

"Ullo, son."

"Ullo, Mum."

"'Ow are yah?"

"Okay."

"'Ow's Cornwall?"

"Still 'ere."

"I 'ope you're be'avin' yourself and eatin' proper."

Silence.

"Now wot about all dem fivers? (Five pound notes.) Where'd 'ey come from?"

"Dunno wotcha talkin' 'bout."

"The money you sent me. All that bread." (Cockney rhyming slang. Bread and Honey. Money.)

"Not me. I didn't send yah no bread."

"Yeah, you did. Fifty ladies. (Cockney rhyming slang. Lady Godivas. Fivers.) Two-'undred and fifty quid." (Quid. Slang for pound sterling.)

Pause.

"Mum, I wanna come 'ome."

"Yeah. Okay, luv. It's quiet 'ere, and a lot of de uvver kids are comin' back. I'll getcha a ticket. 'Ow's next week?"

"Okay."

"And you're sure you don't know nuffin' 'bout all dem fivers?"

"Nah."

"Well, I 'spose I'll 'ang on to 'em for the time bein'. Look after yourself son."

"Bye, Mum."

And so, in the absence of German aerial attacks, Mikey's mother arranged for him to return to London. Many children returned at around the same time, for the same reason. The "Cornish Holiday" he was promised, turned out to be so utterly miserable, that Mikey was understandably delighted to return home. And since his father was away in the army, somewhere in Europe, his mother, who was quite lonely, was equally delighted.

Following their reunion, Mikey and his mother discussed "all dem fivers" many more times, but with no resolution. Meanwhile, "the bread" now resided in a bank account in Mikey's name—for his future. His mother did keep back one five pound note that they spent on a good old fashioned knees-up (slang for a lively party) with family and friends.

Mikey's final suggestion was that, driven by remorse and regret, mean old Meanie McMean slipped a few quid into the envelope—just to make things right.

In your dreams, mate, in your dreams.

The Mean McMeanies
PostScript

As reported in The St. Ives Times
December 15, 1940

Lady Cecilia Smythe-Blenkinsop, Mayor of St. Ives, in the county of Cornwall, recently addressed the full Council of St. Ives:

"As the last of the evacuees leave St. Ives for their homes in London, we are grateful that they, and, I must say, we, all survived what proved to be a most trying time.

"There were pleasurable moments, I'm told, but sadly, too many difficult and stressful times. It is, therefore best, for all concerned, to expedite their return to London. So hurry home, children. Your families await you.

"In conclusion, I wish to add that…."

Before Lady Cecilia could complete her address, a fight erupted, and a number of objects, later shown to be hardened balls of cardboard, were thrown at Council Members. Lady Cecilia and her colleagues briefly defended themselves before they succumbed. It was not determined who threw the first object that knocked Lady Cecilia's flower-festooned hat off her head, but a boy whose name sounded like "bike" was believed to have initiated the violence. Peace was eventually restored, but only when the screaming children left the meeting hall to catch their train back to London.

12

Sleeping Around
PreScript

I heard my mother and her friend talking about a neighborhood teenage girl who they agreed was "sex mad." She slept around, they said. I didn't know what sex mad was exactly, but I decided that must describe me too. After all, I'd been sleeping around a lot. In different shelters. All over London.

Sleeping Around

Script

Air Raid Shelters. Bomb Shelters. Animal Shelters. Means of survival from an aerial attack. A shelter from all that might fall from above. Londoners desperately needed any and all means they could find. And we tried them all.

We quickly learned that the rising and falling wail of an air raid warning was not to be trifled with. On occasion, German bombers arrived before the sound of the siren had faded. It was a message of urgency, and we knew we had to respond immediately. At this moment in my young London life, our brollies—the faithful black umbrella—protected us from whatever usually descended upon us: rain and pigeon crap mostly. But now, different kinds of storm clouds had gathered. And so it rained, not the gentle, glistening droplets of soft rainwater we were used to, but bombs. Bombs of all types, shapes, and sizes, but all with one common purpose: to deliver death and destruction.

Even as a kid, I knew we needed something more robust than an umbrella as protection. Over time, different options emerged. Some good; some bad. To a greater or lesser degree, however, all were vulnerable. There was no guaranteed survival.

The East End of London was not only a geographical part of London, but also an area with its own unique culture. Back then, EastEnders were rough, tough, working-class cockneys. Few of their homes had cellars, so the **Basements** of public buildings and businesses were quickly put to use. Sandbags around entrance ways added additional protection. Dedicated Air Raid Precaution wardens would insist on hustling nearby pedestrians into these facilities as soon as an air raid siren warned us of an imminent attack. As locals, we learned where those shelters were, and could plan our daytime movements accordingly. When the sites were hit by bombs, however, whatever was above the basement, like heavy machinery, would crash through, killing people below. This happened surprisingly often. The safety of a shelter was a relative proposition. Always.

To complement accessible basements, the government quickly constructed above-ground **Street Shelters** made of brick and concrete. But constructed by the government? And quickly? Yeah, right. You can imagine how good and safe those structures were. Even relatively distant explosions could cause them to collapse. On one occasion I remember that my mother and I were caught in a daylight air raid, and we hurried into one of those street shelter sanctuaries. Strange. Very strange. We were the only ones in there. A couple of hours later, the shrill, welcome whine of an "all clear" siren allowed us to leave the shelter and return home. My mother remarked that at least this one was unusually light and airy. "Not as stuffy as usual," she said. I looked back as we walked away, and, smart-arse bugger that I was, pointed out that the structure had no roof. Since many of the street shelters that caved in caused injury and death from collapsing roofs, perhaps this was the new and improved design. We survived, so who knows?

Over time, the public lost confidence in street shelters. *Just because they sometimes collapsed killing everyone huddling there? How fickle can you get?*

So the government provided two popular home shelters. And we had both of them.

Initially, the most popular of these was the **Anderson Shelter.** Nearly four million of them were distributed. And they were free to the less affluent, including us—the even lesser affluent. The shelter came as a do-it-yourself kit, and unassembled, proved to be the most memorable shelter of all. Memorable for me, anyway. I'll tell you why.

Curved and straight panels of galvanized corrugated steel were to be bolted together to form something shaped like a rapidly drawn question mark, lying on the ground, curved side up. They were intended to be buried in four feet of earth and covered with more earth. Unfortunately, in winter,

Anderson shelters were, in essence, cold, damp holes in the ground, and worse, they often flooded in wet weather.

Wet weather? Not exactly an unusual occurrence in the British scheme of things.

Despite their effectiveness in saving lives, spending night after night in a cold, damp hole became less and less appealing.

There was another reason why an outdoor shelter wasn't practical for us. We didn't have enough room for it. We lived in a modest row home. With an even more modest back yard. Not for us, poor working sods that we were, was there usable space. Our backyard was a concrete square that enclosed enough of an earthen center to fill a flower pot. A small flower pot. Far too limited an area to accommodate an Anderson shelter. Fully assembled, it was six feet high, four-and-a half-feet wide, and six-and-a-half feet long.

It was one of those swelteringly hot English summer days, when the temperature may have soared to as high as 70°F. Rosie Davenbury and I were playing in our backyard. The shelter remained unassembled, its component parts lying, waiting patiently on the ground. Curved side up, the panels of the shelter made a great slide. But on that scorcher of a summer's day, the shiny grey metal became uncomfortably hot. After a number of slides, Rosie and I agreed to take our outer clothes off, and cool down in our underpants. She then smiled, and said if I show her mine, she'd show me hers. Was it the friction-induced excitement, or the sight of her milky white thighs? I don't know. But either way, I readily agreed. I was eight years old at the time; she was a little older. Twenty-seven, as I recall. No. Just kidding. Ten, maybe.

With a wrinkled nose, Rosie's immediate comment on seeing Mr. Wiggly, was "Euw, it looks…loose. Like it might fall off. Can it?" I didn't answer. I didn't know. But it was a question that haunted me for a long time.

What I should have replied was that, if it was loose, a little screw would keep it firmly in place! Took me nearly eighty years to think of that!

Rosie's mother and mine were in the kitchen, having tea. After our visitors had gone, I confessed our show-and-show agreement to my mother.

I wonder why I felt the need to *confess*?

"And what did you see?" my mother asked smilingly, teasingly.

Clearly demonstrating my propensity for elegant, descriptive language, coupled with a sharp, anatomically perceptive eye, I replied:

"It was a roundy fing wiv a stripe in the middle." Close enough!

Rosie grew up to be an English teacher, so I can only imagine how she described my fing to 'er muvver.

So much for educational sex and outdoor shelters. Time to come in out of the cold. And damp. Enter the indoor **Morrison Shelter.** Like the Anderson shelter, this too was free for the less affluent, us. It came as a kit consisting of three hundred and fifty-nine parts and several special tools. With skill, patience, and varying degrees of luck, it bolted together to form a steel table six-and-a-half feet long, four feet wide, and two-and-a-half feet high. I should clarify: it didn't do its own bolting, it had to be bolted. And there was the rub: we, primarily my father, apparently had little skill, no patience, but lots of luck—mostly of the bad variety. Properly constructed, it would resemble a steel table with wire mesh sides and a metal mattress base. Even though the instructions were in good English, and not in the now common language of broken foreign, the shelter that my family put together must've been one of the few that had three legs and sloped rather badly. As I recall, we had forty-seven parts left over. Nevertheless, we spent many a night sleeping under there through the worst of the aerial attacks. In retrospect, it was just as well our wobbly safe haven wasn't tested to see how safe it was under fire. We didn't know "safe;" "wobbly," we knew. In lighter moments, few that there seemed to be, I used the steel tabletop as a working surface for my early chemical experiments, and as a war zone for my tin soldiers. By the end of the war, my English army had beaten the German army one hundred and seventeen times—without a loss. Much like our soccer record against Germany. Well, within experimental error, anyway.

As the war continued, especially during the intensive bombing of 1940, we tried all kinds of other shelters. From time to time we huddled under **Railway Arches**. My memory of them is that they always seemed to be cold, damp, and encrusted with the grime of centuries. Perhaps because they were! Constructed of brick, they were frequently old, massive structures, and believed to offered great protection. Not so, apparently. As we were slow to learn, sheltering underneath railway arches was not a particularly good idea: the railway lines above were often targeted by the Germans in their bombing raids.

And so we searched for ever safer shelters, and like threatened moles, we went underground. Deep underground. Networks of long, subterranean **Deep Level Shelters** were constructed beneath some of London's Underground stations; they were capable of holding thousands of people. I thought we'd stay in one of those for a while, but it was not to be. My mother, and apparently many other mothers took issue with them, and took umbrage at the people who managed the facility; they wanted to charge tuppence for a cup of tea. That's two pence per.

Dear American reader, don't try to understand the Brit and his passion for a cuppa. Strong, with milk and sugar. Think of it as satisfying an intense psychological/physiological/biochemical and probably pathological need. But only at a penny a cup. We had our limits.

We opted to seek safety within the **London Underground** transportation system itself, spending many a night sleeping on the platforms of the deeper tube stations; deep was good—most of the time. A quarter of a million people used the London underground as shelters during the Blitz, even though they were still vulnerable to direct hits. As if to prove their vulnerability, hundreds of people were killed while huddled below.

One of our favorite deep level tube stations to spend nights in was nearby Bethnal Green. It was about a mile away, just one short stop down the line from our nearest station, Mile End. Not yet fully functional as a new underground station, it could and often did hold thousands of people. Sadly, one of the most tragic wartime incidents took place at that station.

It was early evening on March 23, 1943. An air raid warning, coupled with nearby artillery explosions, prompted hundreds of people eager to find safety, to enter the station and descend to the platform below via a narrow, ill-lit staircase. They hustled. And they stumbled, pushed, and fell over each other going down the stairs, crushing one hundred and seventy-three people to death. Mostly women and children. One of our neighbors and her young daughter were among those killed in that tragedy. It was the deadliest civilian incident of WWII not directly caused by a German attack. For reasons I'll never know, we'd stopped going to Bethnal Green station a week or so before this tragic event. Divine intervention? I don't think so. I'll opt for an atheist's good fortune based entirely on statistical probability. As I heard many people say many times, after surviving a nearby bomb explosion,

"If it ain't gotchya name on it...."

Initially, the government disallowed the use of platforms as shelters against bombing raids, fearing that people would stay underground all the time; the lack of toilets would then be a significant problem. Generally, Brits obeyed orders. Take spontaneous queueing, for example. But unlike the orderly, order-following Germans, we ignored the rules if we felt we had to. And in seeking the relative safety of an underground station platform, we had to. Personally, I didn't mind subway sleeping at all. It was different, exciting, and I was able to stay up much later than usual. I even got to see a little of my father's father, Grandpa Sam. A gentle man, warm and loving. He joined us on the Piccadilly platform a number of times, when he taught me how to play drafts—checkers to you. He even let me win occasionally.

I liked Grandpa Sam, but apart from sharing a few nights on an underground platform, I didn't know him too well. The Blitz didn't facilitate leisurely family gatherings. He was an old man at the start of the war: seventy at least.

Old, he says? Old? He was seventeen years younger than I am now.

A few years after the war, widower Sam met and married widow Ma B. Her children had already emigrated to Australia. So, after the war, at the age of 77, Grandpa Sam and his new wife joined her kids in Australia. He died in Melbourne a year or so later.

À Propos of grandpas, I didn't know my maternal Grandpa, Grandpa Charlie, at all. He had died before I was born. I was named after him. To digress, again, I should mention that my mother had a thing for English kings and queens. Hence my forenames: Charles and Edward. I always considered myself fortunate to have been born during the reign of a king and not a queen. Who knows, I could have been called Elizabeth Victoria.

Grandpa Charlie and I were linked in another way. During those wartime years, the functional and iconic red, double-decker London bus was one of the few colorful objects in our dark and colorless lives. Rubble, after all, is a dull, dusty, gray-brown. Growing up in London, the double-decker was my principal source of transport. Number 10 or 25 was a direct ride to and from London's West End, the city's entertainment center. I loved sitting in the front row, upper deck, right above the driver, feeling the bus zoom and sway through the narrow streets of London. Later, as a student, I'd discovered that the famous German chemist Kekulé, better known to his buds as Friedrich August Kekulé von Stradonitz, while seated on the top of a London bus, had visions that led him to the theory of aromaticity, a major slice of organic chemistry. Many years before, I too was drawn to study that fascinating science.

How did Grandpa Charlie fit into the London bus story? Well, he really fitted *under* rather than into it. A few years before I was born, poor Charlie was knocked down by a London bus and was trapped, alive, beneath it. After considerable effort, they were able to raise one end of the bus intending to pull him out. Sadly, the device gave way and the bus fell back on Grandpa—tragically killing him outright. Grandpa Charlie, Kekulé, and I were thereafter forever linked to each other via the old, faithful, red double-decker London bus.

So yes, in sum, we had all kinds of shelters protecting us from death-distributing German bombers like the Heinkels, Dorniers, Focke-Wulfs, and Junkers. But Londoners had other arrows in their quiver, essential components that protected and sustained us like no others. Yes, they're worth mentioning again, factors that the Nazi bastards could never fully comprehend: a sense of humor, a strong cuppa char, and our Winnie.

Sleeping Around
PostScript

One type of shelter that was effectively non-existent in WWII's East End of London was that of the religious shelter. Of any faith. Rarely did my neighborhood or school friends ever mention houses of worship being relevant in their lives, whether they offered physical or spiritual support. Not surprising perhaps. The secularization of Great Britain began nearly a hundred years earlier, during and after World War I. And it's been gathering momentum ever since. Britain is now among the least religious countries in the world, where fifty percent of its citizens are nonbelievers. At its current rate of change, it's projected that by the year 2067, Christians in Britain will be statistically invisible. In comparison, while still under considerable debate, it's estimated that twenty-five percent of the US population are nonbelievers.

And a sad note: I recently learned that London's dou-ble-decker bus will in future no longer be diesel powered, spewing black exhaust into the London air; it is to be an all-electric design: smooth, quiet, and eco-friendly. No lon-ger will it contribute to the smog-ridden air of London's yesteryear.

Strange: I miss a good, old-fashioned pea-souper.

13

War Stuff

PreScript

Great Britain declared war on Germany in September, 1939. As you might imagine, it was *the* topic of conversation. What was going to happen, and when? We talked about it at home, in school, and among ourselves. Everyone was expecting immediate action—of some kind. Would we be attacked by Germany? Would we attack first? Listening to these conversations as a young boy, my pals and I became impatient for something to happen. We were ready. Ready to fight. Ready to fight back. Or fight forward. A good sense of direction was rare in London. It was also of limited use.

Not much happened initially. Or seemingly for ever. A few isolated incidents were reported, but nothing to affect us directly. Then, nearly a year after the war formally began, on September 7, 1940, the German Air Force came to call.

And outstayed their welcome by eight months. From then on my collection of "war stuff" was assured.

Perhaps I should summarize my collecting skills and experience. To be honest, I hadn't been much of a collector: a few stamps and one or two coins here and there. That's it. Since I didn't receive a regular allowance of any kind, buying objects to collect wasn't really an option. And in my concrete world, there weren't many collectibles available of a natural origin. The nearest plant life was in Victoria Park, about three miles away. Too far, for an unaccompanied little kid to visit. It also meant crossing a major road. The only other "unconcretized" area that was somewhat accessible was Tower Hamlets Cemetery at the bottom of the street. We did consider this to be a good source for a bone collection, but the graveyard was surrounded by a forbidding iron fence that was particularly tough to climb. The old, overgrown, crumbling gravestones weren't exactly inviting either.

If I was good at collecting anything, it was gathering unusual stones that I'd find in the area. Or ones that were thrown at me during the many stone fights we'd have with kids invading us from other streets.

So I hope you're convinced that I had well-honed collecting skills, and that I was ready for the real stuff.

War Stuff
Script

During the Battle of Britain, the British defense system con-sisted of many components: plane spotters, fighter planes, anti-aircraft artillery, searchlights, radar, barrage balloons, shelters, sandbags, emergency vehicles, Air Raid Precau-tion Wardens, gas masks, blackouts, and evacuation. Most proved to be critically necessary at different stages of the war.

We also had two other uniquely British weapons: one was the leadership of Winston Churchill and his silver-tongued eloquence—an inspiring orator despite, or because of, his speech impediments. Winnie was that rare man of letters who, it seemed, even wrote with a lisp!

And, especially during the Blitz, perhaps the most important weapon of all, the unshakeable spirit of the Lon-don people. Confidence? Cockiness? Whatever the label, it was effective.

To a young EastEnder, already socio-economically confined by few travel opportunities, the war imposed additional limitations. The rare day trip to the seaside, about forty miles, was out; there were fewer school trips, movies, trips to local parks, and bus and underground rides around London. With minimal warning time for air raids, or even no warning at all, kids were kept on an unusually tight leash. Including me. This was survival time.

Travel restrictions like these seemed to make collecting things more difficult, and of greater importance—a link with the outside world, perhaps. Further, since my collectibles were war-related, I felt that I'd met some deep-seated need to be involved. Anyway, it was Churchill's fault: he was always saying we all had to "do our bit." I wasn't sure which bit I should be doing, but in any event, this was mine.

I called my collection of Blitz-related memorabilia my "War Stuff."

As I mentioned earlier, I was a precocious bastard. Even at that tender age, I had an obvious flair for descriptive phraseology. This was another example. Like the roundy fing?

The principal sources of my collectibles were barrage balloons, anti-aircraft artillery, bombs, and bits of aircraft. Here's how.

Early in the Blitz, when London was being heavily bombed, German dive bombers were striking their objectives with relative ease. Anti-aircraft guns couldn't effectively track planes flying at low altitude and high-speed. Enter the Barrage Balloon, designed to protect cities and key targets. We called 'em blimps. Over time, about 3,000 balloons were deployed throughout the UK, with 500 or so positioned over London at a height of about 5,000 feet. No longer able to dive bomb, the planes were forced to fly at higher altitudes, with less bombing precision. They were then far more vulnerable to anti-aircraft fire.

From below, those puffy protectors seemed almost soft and cuddly. Covered in silver fabric, the hydrogen-filled blimps were stabilized in windy conditions by steel cables; attached to winches, they were moved around on trucks. If a plane made contact with a balloon, or its attached cable, the result was usually one less plane to worry about. I remember seeing that happen a few times; we cheered when it did.

The balloons were sixty-two feet long. For my American friends, if you're having a hard time picturing that length, think of the distance between the two wickets on a cricket pitch—and subtract four feet.

The AcAc, the anti-aircraft artillery, fired shells that were designed to explode into a cloud of steel fragments which, if near enough to enemy aircraft, could bring them down. The steel fragments that fell to the ground were the primary source of my shrapnel collection.

Thank you, Major General Henry Shrapnel, for inventing the exploding shell. I'd have had much less to collect without your contribution.

My War Stuff consisted of four shoeboxes: Box Number One was for "Odds and Sods," the cockney term for miscellaneous. It held my foreign stamp collection—all seven of which were American; my military souvenirs, consisting of a tag that said "US Army" that my GI friend, Billy Joe, gave me; and an American quarter representing my foreign coin hoard.

Can one coin constitute a hoard?

In addition, there was a gold button which, for reasons I no longer remember, I *knew* was from the uniform of a German general. I traded two large pieces of shrapnel for a tiny piece of hard, black rubber. An older boy, an experienced hustler, convinced me that he actually saw it fall from the front tire of a burning German bomber. That kid was destined for a job in sales; clearly, I wasn't. Finally, there was a small heart-shaped stone that I'd found before the war; I had nowhere else to keep it.

Box Number Two contained many pieces of silver blimp fabric, some quite charred. Those cuddly bubbles in the sky had sacrificed their lives in the downfall of enemy planes.

One could ask for no more…of the blimps or the planes.

Boxes Three and Four were devoted entirely to shrapnel—my prized possession. One of the big advantages of living in the East End—at least as I saw it—was that we were often at the center of an air raid. As a result, we had a goodly share of the metal fragments that fell to earth. Following a heavy, nighttime raid, the whole area could be littered with shrapnel. That's when we "bigger" boys took to the streets, cleaning up like vultures after the kill. At seven years of age, I might not have been "big," but I was experienced. In any event, there was certainly no need for the authorities to take care of the job. It was our tacitly assigned task to gather up those viciously sharp, jagged fragments of shells and bombs that were often still warm. Even uncomfortably hot at times.

Box Three was full of those pieces of metal, and many a cut and bleeding hand proved that I had personally gathered them; I had done my share of vulturing. Yes, a glove would have been a good idea, but this was no activity for sissies. This was war! And boxes three and four proved that. Especially Box Four.

I was fascinated by the daylight bombing of London, and by the many dogfights that took place; they were my ultimate wartime thrill. My early experiences, however, quickly changed my understanding of those busy skies. On one particular morning I yielded to the temptation to "nip out" (BritSpeak, meaning to leave and return quickly—not to be confused with "Nip Out," a product that claims to enhance a woman's nipple size and "perkiness")…to nip out and take a quick look at the action. Before Dear Mama could drag me back into the house, I was able to collect an "extrasuperspecial" piece of shrapnel. A small fragment had ricocheted off the side of the house, and found its way into the fleshy part of my left calf muscle. I remember that it hurt like hell. But only briefly. That piece of metal, covered in blood, my blood, rested proudly in Box Four. It was the envy of all my friends, and an early lesson for me in how the prize could overcome the pain.

Despite that early experience, I remained determined to bypass parental controls whenever I could, and observe aerial warfare in the flesh, so to speak. My flesh, I guess. I later learned that falling shrapnel, from friendly shells or from enemy bombs, could seriously injure or even kill people. Knowing this only increased the value of my bloody souvenir—to my way of thinking, anyway. And treating my "war wound" as a badge of honor, I kept sticky plaster (an adhesive bandage) on my leg for weeks, well after the healing process was complete. I just hoped the scar would last forever. Sadly, it didn't.

If I'd have shown a little more creativity, Box 5 could have contained my mother's carefully recorded, shorthand versions of Churchill's speeches. Even with my limited trading skills, they should have been good for bartering at the very least.

Even at the age of seven, I knew that other objects fell from the sky during those many raids: bits of German planes; bits of Germans. Inevitably, sadly, there were also fragments of British planes and pilots.

Too many of ours; not enough of theirs.

There were dead and dying people amid the rubble. The morning after a night raid was the time we'd quietly watch the rescue of people buried beneath collapsed houses, or the recovery of what was left of them. We quickly developed an immunity to the horrors that surrounded us. It was only many years later, and again as I now recall the images and feelings, that I see those events through the eyes of an adult. They were a lot easier to accept as a young boy.

From innocence to worldliness; from fun to fear.

War Stuff
PostScript

Damn. I should've kept my War Stuff collection. I could have had "told wealth"—and *I'd* be doing the telling. Take Kevin Wheatcroft in Leicestershire, England, for example. His collection of German military vehicles and Nazi memorabilia is widely regarded as the world's largest. It's been valued at over $160 million. Who knows? We could have merged our two collections into something really spectacular.

The phenomenon of "Children of the Blitz" collecting shrapnel in World War II has been studied in recent years by serious academic investigators. Modern-day archeologists, like Dr. Gabriel Moshenska of University College in London. He and his academic colleagues suggest that "Collecting can be a coping mechanism for children in traumatic environments...based on an understanding of collecting both as a social practice and as a process of order-ing and controlling chaotic material culture…for children, collecting is a rudimentary way of mastering the outside world, of arranging, classifying and manipulating."

Then again, perhaps there was a simpler explanation: in pre-war times, we had little opportunity to collect anything. Now, there were all kinds of souvenirs falling from the sky. And they were free. Further, it was always competitive to grab them before other kids could. That, of course, added to their desirability. As did the risk of bleeding in the gath-ering process.

Latter-day archeologists conclude that "Virtually no aspect of society is untouched by war, and yet so far there has been very little consideration of the ways in which children have encountered and interacted with the material culture of modern conflicts. Examining the things that children collect and curate can reveal unexpected details of their sensory perceptions of the world around them, their experiences and memories embodied in and represented by objects."

Right on. And what do I say as one of the Children of the Blitz, one of the collectors? I had no idea that I was such a perceptive seven-year-old.

Mastering the outside world?

Wow. I'm impressed. No one told me that before.

14

Oberstleutenant Wolfgang Schmidt
PreScript

The Nazi government had warned all German soldiers about the dangers of being captured alive by the British.

"A fate worse than death," they warned.

And what would a fate worse than death be for a German in the hands of the British? A last meal of Beans on Toast, that's what!

Oberstleutenant Wolfgang Schmidt Script

A major thrust of the Battle of Britain was the ruthless bombing of London. Air raids targeting both strategic objectives and civilian populations were carried out night and day. All too frequently, vast numbers of German bombers would spew their venom over London. On September 7, 1940, almost 1000 German aircraft, more than 300 bombers escorted by 600 fighters, filled the sky. The largest number of aircraft ever seen virtually blocked out the sun. The spectacular dogfight that developed over London that day was awe-inspiring. Picture it if you can. Maybe you can't. Perhaps you had to be there. I was.

During the daylight raids, the British anti-aircraft guns were quiet, allowing British fighter planes, the remarkably maneuverable Hurricanes and Spitfires, to engage the enemy. With hundreds of German bombers above, it was hard to believe that all their bombs could miss us. But they did. I'm here. I survived. And I remember.

The bombers were escorted by fighter planes like the Messerschmidt. For a young boy to witness the spectacle of dogfights taking place in broad daylight, right above where he lived, was nothing short of sensational. For me, this was one of the most exciting memories of the war. The fire-fueled orange skies, the black smoke of death and destruction that quickly formed, the dark specs of bombs raining down from those sodding gits above, all left their indelible memories.

Monstrous machines that appeared to be giving birth to tiny, evil offspring, which in turn gave birth to death.

For that naive seven-year-old, these weren't memories of fear, but memories of excitement! Mortality wasn't an issue. For the adults around me, it was, of course, different. I could sense their fear. But it was their fear. Not mine.

On one unusually sunny morning, the heavy drone of a sky full of threatening death was palpable. Oppressive. Fighters, theirs and ours, were zooming high and low, zigzag-ging across the sky. A Spitfire was chasing a Messerschmidt. Black smoke was streaming from the German's tail. And that was something to remember. So I did. The German plane suddenly started to shake violently, and amid a screeching descent, twisted and turned its way down to earth. It crashed in the next street over from ours. Even though I thought I was prepared for the sound of the impact, I wasn't. The boom was deafening. Even the ground shook. I looked up to the sky again to see a parachute gently floating down as it followed the same path as the plane. I quickly lost sight of it in the fiery, dense, black smoke that was rising up to meet it. I wondered if the pilot would choke to death on the smoke and flames from his own plane. I ran to the next street over where I thought the crash occurred in time to see the last of the flames die out. As if in its death throes, the propeller continued to turn until it sputtered to a halt. A smoldering tangle of twisted metal was all that remained. There was no obvious sign of the pilot anywhere.

A neighbor of ours, who, like my father, was both too old and/or unfit to serve in the armed forces, was a dedicated Air Raid Precaution warden. He ushered those of us who'd gathered to watch out of harm's way. I ran back to where I lived, the patriotically named British Street, to share the excitement "wiv me mates."

I climbed over the barrier intended to keep us out of Number 28. As I mentioned earlier, it was now the shell of a bombed house that became our private meeting place. Yes, the walls might collapse at any moment, but so what. That added an extra thrill. We were British, and made of sterner stuff! At least, that's what Churchill told us. And kept telling us. In any event, it was where my pals and I made all our plans to fight the Nazi bastards. To be serious about this, and to enter the grown-up mode, we smoked our pretend cigarettes of rolled up brown paper.

Another vivid memory—and a bloody awful one it still is!

On this occasion I was in the basement, waiting for the rest of the gang to join me. We usually got together after a daylight raid. I was rolling a brown paper special, when I heard a soft noise that sounded like a cross between a gurgle and a groan; it came from somewhere in the shadows. I checked. Behind a pile of cardboard boxes and old clothes, I discovered a man, in uniform, lying face down.

Two days earlier, my friends and I had speculated on what we'd do if we captured a German airman who had bailed out over London.

Tony was unequivocally sure of his course of action: "Kick 'im in the balls!"

Donald's suggestion was: "Bang a nail into his arse!"

I didn't think he'd thought that through too well.

Mine was perhaps more pragmatic: "'it 'im over the 'ead wiv a big piece of wood. Wham! Bam! Pow! Then tie 'im up, and get 'elp."

So, to that degree, we had a plan. The man's arms were lying loosely by his side. Since I didn't have to knock him out, I looked around for some rope, string, anything to tie him up with. There was none, of course. Our plans only went so far. I then remembered that I had a tangled mess of licorice string in my pocket. This was my "sweets" allowance for the week. To use it to tie up a prisoner was good for the health of my teeth, not so good as a means of restraint. But it was string, and it was all I had. I tied the man's hands together behind him. He started to stir.

"Friend or Foe?" I asked. Since I didn't actually know what a "foe" was, I hoped he'd say "friend."

With obvious difficulty, he staggered to his feet. For a seven-year-old, I was small for my age. He was tall for his, and towered over me. Since he didn't look too friendly, or too British, I played it safe. I took out my "SuperSpecial Warrior Catapult," quickly loaded it with a small stone, and pointed it at him, ready to fire.

"Stick 'em up!" I snapped.

He frowned, and then smiled. In perfect English, he almost whispered, "Well, that's going to be difficult. My hands are tied behind me."

"Well," I said, "OK. Just don't move."

I couldn't help noticing that he was bleeding from a head wound, and the left leg of his pants was soaked in blood. A trickle of the red stuff ran down from the corner of his mouth. His black Iron Cross, proudly hanging around his neck, was more red than black.

I later wondered whether this was a clever scheme for him to claim he was in the *Red* Cross. By "later," I mean much later—a few weeks ago, in fact.

"You've got me covered," he said.

"Just don't move, or I'll 'ave to shootcha wiv me caterpillar," I replied.

"You mean, catapult, don't you?"

"Yeah, dat's what I meant to say."

He looked down at me...way down, and said, "Could be a remake of David and Goliath."

"'Oo?"

He brushed my question aside, and asked, "So, what do you plan to do with me?"

"I'm takin' you to the Police Station."

"PlayStation? Why would you take me there?" he asked.

What the 'ell is 'e talkin' about? I was too young; he was too German; and PlayStations were too far off in the future to make sense of this exchange.

The German chortled. Strange. Brits chortle. Germans never chortle. In fact, Germans don't even say "chortle." Their word is "glucksen," and that says it all. In German. Nevertheless, it was a pun to remember. And I did. For the rest of my life.

"All right," he said, "but first let me introduce myself. I am Oberstleutnant Wolfgang Schmidt." I didn't hear the click of his heels then, but I do now. With that, he brought his arms forward, scarcely aware that he was snapping my licorice string. He held out his hand to shake mine. I instinctively took his.

"You know, you'll probably get a medal for my capture. I'm the top pilot in the Luftwaffe, that's the German Air Force. You'll be a big hero."

Wow, I thought. *A medal, eh? Yeah, I'd like that.* In fact, I was chuffed. Dead chuffed.

He smiled, and asked, "Am I your first POW?"

Since I didn't know what a POW was, I just shrugged.

"Follow me," I said, full of newly acquired confidence.

He shook his head. "Wait. I don't want to tell you how to do your job, but if I'm your prisoner, perhaps I should go first. What do you think?"

"Yeah, okay. You go first. I'll follow you. But no funny stuff."

"Wouldn't dream of it."

We climbed out of the basement of Number 28 and started to walk towards Mile End Road. Within a few feet, he stumbled, made a strange, high-pitched, whining sound, and, as if in slow motion, slumped to the ground.

Now what? I didn't expect that. I was wondering what to do next when the shrill whine of the siren penetrated my muddled mind. I looked up at an unfamiliar ceiling, and slowly realized I was lying in a bunk in the community air raid shelter. The one at the end of British Street.

I felt a gentle hand on my shoulder. It was my mother's. "Wake up, dear. That's the All Clear siren. We can go home now."

It took me a few more moments to gather my thoughts. Too many nights of sleep interrupted by air raids took their toll.

It was early morning when we emerged. I squinted at the unusually bright sunshine in the unusually bright, clear blue sky. No signs of enemy planes there. Good, I could concentrate on the important work I had to do. I checked my pockets: the catapult was there, but my licorice string was gone. I then remembered I'd eaten it the night before.

Later that day, I found a piece of string nearly two feet long, and placed it carefully in my back pocket with my catapult. This time, I was ready to take my first real prisoner. Then again, perhaps I should let Tony and Donald soften him up first.

Oberstleutnant Wolfgang Schmidt PostScript

Let's consider the implications of this dream of mine. A typical boyhood wish to be a hero? I asked professional "Dream Analysts" to interpret my dream. Here's what they said:

"To dream of war-related events wasn't surprising; they represent a threat to your existence."

Yes, my existence was certainly threatened.

"A plane reflects the direction our life is taking, and how much control we have. To dream of a plane crashing meant I felt danger. That my survival was in doubt."

Really? I was in the middle of a bloody war, and under attack. Of course my survival was in doubt!

"Seeing the enemy as a big man, towering over me, showed the enemy to be a powerful force."

Yep. It sure was.

"Dealing with them represented an attempt to resolve a life problem."

Right. We call it life or death.

"To dream about string, licorice string in my case, showed concern about my ability to hold the situation together."

Yes, I was aware of having little control of the war. Wonder why?

"Encountering the enemy in a basement represents what has been neglected, or what the dreamer is not aware of in his waking life."

You mean, there really was a German pilot hiding down there?

15

The Yanks Are Coming. Aren't They?
PreScript

"Sure we want to go home. We want this war over with.
The quickest way to get it over with is to go get the
bastards who started it."

George S. Patton
General, US Army

As Britain struggled for survival, and year two of the war
drifted depressingly into year three, so hope for a bright future, or a future of any kind, dwindled. A German invasion
seemed to be inevitable. It was as if the rest of the world
had succumbed to the Nazis. Certainly, all of our European
neighbors had. We were more alone than ever. But, urged
on by our indomitable leader, we continued to fight. Winnie

remained committed to victory, and where Winnie went, we followed.

Despite his persuasive powers, Churchill failed to convince America to enter WWII. It was seemingly not to be. And many Brits believed that if America waited much longer, it might well be too late to save us. Ironically, it took Japan's cowardly attack on Pearl Harbor on December 7, 1941, President Roosevelt's "date that will live in infamy," to provoke the US into war. On the following day, America formalized its rightful place in the world conflict. The UK enthusiastically welcomed them.

I was just nine years old at the time—old enough to recognize the pervasive sense of intense *relief*. Relief that you could cut with a samurai sword. The word, "finally!" was on everyone's lips. *Finally*, we had an ally. A powerful ally. And *finally* questions of our ability to survive quickly morphed into a belief in our ultimate victory. The heavy clouds of inevitable doom were lifting. We suddenly had a future.

I didn't know it at the time, but had the US *not* entered the war there was a good chance that I might not be here writing about it in 2019. A very good chance.

The Yanks Are Coming. Aren't They?
Script

When I first heard that the Yanks were coming to London, I was excited. Based on my knowledge of Americans from "the pictures" (movies), they'd surely all be cowboys and G-men: ready to fight, ready to shoot, and ready to win. Just what we needed.

Three million GIs passed through the UK during World War II. I didn't meet all of them, but I do remember some. With warmth and affection.

The GIs who poured into London were generally thought of as friendly, outgoing, generous and, compared to the British soldier, rich. Not surprisingly, they quickly became enormously popular with both young women and kids. Not so, however, with the young British soldier; he was typically away from home fighting the enemy somewhere else. The popular phrase: "Overpaid, Oversexed, and Over There," wasn't always used with affection and humor. Personally, I was delighted having them around: sure they were friendly, but more importantly, they always seem to have candy to share. Remember, I was a longtime candy-deprived kid in a perpetual state of withdrawal. My one disappointment was that the GIs I came to know weren't wearing six-shooters; I'm sure if they were, they'd have taught me how to use 'em.

Tony and I were at the Tower Hamlets Cemetery end of British Street, deeply immersed in a game of conkers. Seemingly unaware of us and where he was walking, a tall, pale-faced GI was fully absorbed comparing street signs with a map he was holding. Visiting old cemeteries was apparently a passion of his, and, with its old and crumbling gravestones dating back to the early eighteen hundreds, Tower Hamlets was high on his list.

Coming upon us rather abruptly, he stopped, smiled warmly, and drawled a "Howdy."

How D? I thought. *Wassat mean?*

His, "I'm Bob," was even more peculiar: no English adult would ever introduce himself to strange kids using his first name.

He quickly became interested in our game. "What are you guys playing?"

Not very attentive is he. Didn't he read my earlier comment that we were "deeply immersed in a game of conkers"?

I'll tell 'im again, I thought. "Playin' conkers," I said.

He frowned, and asked," How do you do that?"

I explained. "You make an 'ole in an 'orse chestnut. Put a piece of string fru it, and make a big knot at the end. Then 'old up your conker, while the uvver kid swings 'is and 'its yours. Then it's your turn. And you keep takin' turns till one of 'em breaks. If we're bofe usin' new conkers, and mine wins, then my conker becomes a one-er. If I break Tony's seven-er, then my one-er becomes an eight-er. I 'ad a firteen-er once."

The combination of a strange game explained in a strange cockney accent was clearly something of a challenge to Bob. 'E should 'ear me explanation of cricket!

Bob would have been fascinated to learn that the game of conkers in England dated back nearly two hundred years. I couldn't tell him at the time; I didn't find that out until I started to write this chapter.

Quite suddenly, Tony blurted out, "Got any gum, chum?" We London kids had quickly learned to ask that of all the American soldiers.

Patting his pockets, Bob said, "Sure. Got a packet of Wrigley's somewhere."

"Wrigglies?" I repeated, a little shocked. "Like *worms?*" I asked, fearing the worst. How little I knew. Over time, I came to love Wrigley's Juicy Fruit gum, even years later when rationing was a thing of the past.

As we all chomped down on our sticks of Wrigley's, our gum-giving friend asked, "How far is it to Mile End Station?"

I replied, "Not far."

"Which direction?"

I pointed. "That way."

"I'm a little turned around," he said, looking up at the gray, sun-starved sky for help denied: is that north? South? East? West?"

"I d'know." I didn't explain, and probably couldn't. In our part of London, the little side streets twisted, turned, and doubled back on themselves. Finding one's way using points of the compass, was relatively fruitless. *Juicy Fruitless.* To go north, you may well have to start by heading due east, continuing south, before heading north; then east again. Typical US towns weren't founded in 43 AD, as London was.

He gave up on direction and tried distance. "How many blocks?"

"'Ow many blocks?" I repeated, in my own style. "Blocks of what?"

I thought I'd better end this conversation; it was getting to be too confusing. Before Bob could comment further, I quickly added, "I d'know."

The streets of old London could, at best, be described as organized chaos—except they weren't very organized. The notion of blocks had no relevance.

Much later, I came to understand what Churchill meant when he said: "Great Britain and the United States, two nations separated by a common language." Or did Bernard Shaw say it? Who knows? Well, I do know that *I* said it. I just wasn't the *first* to say it.

"You know," Bob said, "I just came from your southern coast. They've removed all the signs showing where and how far the towns are from each other."

"Why'd they do that?" I asked.

Bob shrugged. "Well, I guess they want to complicate things for the Germans if they invade England. But you know, from what I've seen here, you at least don't need to remove the London street signs: they won't help the Germans at all. In fact, leave them in; they'll do a great job of confusing them."

As a matter of fact, they never did remove the London street signs.

The Kings Arms was an old pub, even by London standards. It was at the top end of British Street. At the bottom end was Tower Hamlets Cemetery. I now wonder whether it was in any way symbolic that we lived smack dab between the two. The locals called them Heaven and Hell. Well, actually 'Eaven and 'Ell. They never told me which was which.

It was a relatively quiet Sunday. Donald, Tony, Chris, and I were playing football (that's soccer to you) at the pub end of the street, when Tony's big sister, Jacqueline, stumbled out of the pub, trying to separate two GIs, one hefty white man, and one skinny black. I was fascinated: the skinny guy was the first black man I'd ever seen. The men were shouting and pushing each other, using swear words I'd never heard before. Frankly, I was surprised: I thought I knew them all. From my early years, I already had a pretty good vocabulary. That's to say, a pretty bad vocabulary.

I once heard it said that the first three words a cockney kid learns are: Mum, Fuck, and Dad. In that order. And by the way, that's "Mum" and not "Mom."

Both GIs seemed to be yelling about the other's mother, which I didn't understand. As the yelling became louder, and the pushing and shoving turned to hitting with closed fists, the white soldier pulled a vicious looking knife and began to threaten his compatriot. A few of the locals gathered around the black GI to protect him. A bobby (policeman) suddenly appeared, and managed to calm things down.

What a pity that the soldiers weren't wearing guns, I thought. *They could have had a shootout on British Street. Boy, life with the GIs was proving to be exciting. I was glad they were…over here. With or without Wrigley's gum.*

Before the war, there were just a few thousand blacks scattered around the UK. British Commonwealth citizens mostly. A white woman on the arm of a black man might have prompted a raised eyebrow, but in general, there were few obvious signs of bigotry. British intolerance to black GIs was negligible. There were a few recorded instances when upper-class gits vocalized their disgust at having to share shelters with blacks, whether GIs or not. In point of fact, they also resented having to mix with the poor—the hoi polloi. In the East End, however, where we had no "personages of privilege," all was peaceful and quiet. As far as I knew, anyway…

From pictures I'd seen in comic books, Billy Joe looked like a black Charles Atlas. "Mr. Muscles," as I called him, was a guest of the family. My mother's sister, and one or two more distant English relatives of ours, had emigrated to the US many years earlier. To places like New York, Chicago, and Los Angeles. They'd mention us to any young American soldier who might find himself in London, and urged them to visit. Those who were especially lonely jumped at the chance of spending time with a British family, and enjoying a home-cooked meal, however modest it inevitably would be. Knowing that food was heavily rationed, they always brought goodies like coffee, sugar—and candy for me. And these weren't my old favorites, like Jelly Babies, Sherbet Dabs, and Gobstoppers, but the new world, new wave Snickers, Oh Henrys, and Baby Ruths. That's what they were talking about! And they knew of what they spoke.

After all this talk about candy, you may be wondering what condition my teeth were in. They were in great condition—at least the ones I had left were. During those war years, a we're-too-busy-to worry-about oral hygiene, disrupted access to dental care, and a European attitude of extract 'em and forget 'em, all conspired to leave me missing several teeth by the end of the war. I was twelve.

Billy Joe was from Chattanooga. When he told me that, I thought he'd made the name up; it sounded so funny. I laughed. He didn't. It became less strange when the song Chattanooga Choo-Choo gained so much popularity at the time.

Billy Joe treated me like his kid brother, teaching me many things about America. Baseball was one of his favorite topics; he hoped to become a professional player when the war was over. On a subsequent visit, he brought me a gift, a real American baseball.

"It's autographed by Ted Williams," he said, "And that makes it very special."

"Oh? 'Oo's Ted Williams?"

I can still feel the mixture of his surprise and disappointment.

I treasured that ball, but sadly it was lost during a subsequent air-raid.

Before he left the UK for duties elsewhere, Billy Joe made me promise to visit him in Chattanooga, or "Nooga" as he called it. I live in Sarasota, Florida, now; only a few hours away. I could drive there, and look up old Billy Joe. And yes, he would be *Old* Billy Joe; a hundred or more. Trouble is, I have no idea what his last name is, and there just might be more than one Billy Joe in Tennessee.

The Yanks Are Coming. Aren't They?
PostScript

By the end of the war, the more than three million GIs who had passed through the UK had left their marks. Good and bad.

Only in recent years has it come to light that there were, throughout the UK, many fights between black and white GIs, some of the brawls developing into near-riots. Insisting on the segregation that their local communities practiced back in the US, white GIs tried, unsuccessfully, to have the blacks banned from bars, clubs, and cinemas. Clear abuse of black soldiers by the US Military Police was frequently reported. Many ordinary Brits, in a strong showing of support, physically protected black victims, often welcoming them into their homes.

During the 3 years of their stay, GIs committed 26 murders, 31 manslaughters, 22 attempted murders, and more than 400 sexual offenses, including 126 rapes. Nine thousand war babies were born out of wedlock. Not a record to be proud of, to be sure. On the other side of the ledger, 70,000 British women became GI brides.

In myriad ways, life for the Brits would never again be the same. Nor, probably, for the 3 million GIs. In the world of chemistry, we call it hybridisation or, under the circumstances, hybridization, depending on which side of the pond you're on.

Over the decades my admiration for the GIs I met during those war years has grown; without their sacrifices, I might never have survived. So I thank, salute, and honor them. Over 400,000 American servicemen and women failed to return to the US. I hope that Billy Joe, Bob, Jonny, and the others I came to know defied the odds and made it back home. I'll never know. But that's what I want to believe.

16

Nellie and the Nazis
PreScript

They were sending me away. Far away. Away from home. Away from London. To the distant town of Frome (pronounced Froom), a peaceful little place in the county of Somerset, population about ten thousand. A hundred miles west of London. I'd never been that far from home. Nor had I ever been away on "me jack" either. "Jack?" That's cockney rhyming slang for "own." As in Jack "Jone(s)."

Was I a little scared? Nah. A lot scared, maybe. But we EastEnders were born to be tough. So I feigned confidence, even though my feigning skills were limited. So I told everyone I was excited and ready to go. This was going to be fun. An adventure to remember. And I tried hard to believe it.

Why Frome? Because that's where Coopers' Company's School, my grammar school, had relocated to from London. Frankly, I'd never heard of Frome before, and I had a vague idea that Somerset might be a separate country. Keep in mind that, to a Londoner leading an exclusive intraLondon existence, Piccadilly Circus wasn't just the hub of London, it was the hub of the universe. So Frome was just like Manchester, Birmingham, Scotland, or Wales. All irrelevantly "outside" somewhere.

Arrogant bastards these Londoners.

The event that precipitated my parents' Somerset decision was a particularly devastating and sustained air raid over London. We were huddled under our Morrison shelter set up in the living room. Comforting to know that it was called the "living room." You'll recall that the Morrison shelter was a huge steel table that the government issued to protect us. That night, in response to a powerful explosion that destroyed a neighbor's house, our house shook violently. Wall cracks appeared. Windows shattered. An eerie cacophony of howling dogs filled the after-explosion silence. Leaving London for a while made good sense.

On the day I left, all air raids over London ceased. And stayed "ceased" for the whole of the time I was in Somerset. Earlier, we'd spent a short time in Guildford, Surrey. Same outcome: nothing happened to London while we were somewhere else. My parents obviously had an uncanny sense of timing, an ability to predict impending attacks by the enemy. I'm being sarcastic, of course. But since my whole family managed to live through the war, I can't be too critical. I must remind myself that we did achieve our primary objective: survival.

So I was ready for the green hills of Somerset. Still suspicious that Somerset might be "foreign," however, I asked my English teacher what language they spoke there. He smiled, knowingly, and warned me that the Somerset dialect might be quite a challenge for me to understand. He gave me "Zummut Vrom Zummerzet," a humorous poem by Outis, to introduce us to the local lingo.

Light Yer Vire Upon Tha Top

Ther's a maxim wuth tha tryin, in yer piaper
I've a read it,
Tull siave yer caul ef not yer biacon (twer vrom
a biacon shop);
Ef yo wants ta pass the winter in comfort and
in credit,
Kip a vire and kip a good un, but light un
on the top.

In tha bottom of yer griate, laay of cauls a
good voundation;
Pack um as thaw twar aggs, thaw a little time
it hinders

(You'll siave tha time hereaater as you spends
in preparaition),
Then, on tha top of aal, pile yer straa and
sticks and zinders.

And very zoon thay catches, athout a wiastin
o yer matches;
And, when a vire es laaid thic waay, a doant
want ner a stoaker,
Vor tull burn athout no poakin, and wi very
little smoakin,
Zo you mid burn tha billuses and tiake awaay
the poaker.

My missus tried it on about twenty years agone.
You must light tha vire a nour or zo, afore ull
get hot droo;
But aaterwards you'll get no smother, but girt
yeat,
And tull you miake one ton o caul goo mooast
as vur as two.

With those words ringing discordantly in my ears, I was
suddenly feeling much less confident about my ability to
manage life in Frome. My feigns were weakening.

Nellie and the Nazis
Script

Coopers' Company's School, my new grammar school, was originally located in Bow, a ten-minute bike ride from where I lived. But early in the war, the staff and students were evacuated to Frome, in Somerset. I was about eleven years old when I spent a couple of months there, once again during a time totally devoid of air raids over London.

The train ride from London to Frome in Somerset was to be my first big trip alone. Surprisingly, there was no typical fine drizzle that morning; instead, it poured. My mother, who took me to Paddington Station, was worried. For several reasons. One was that she always worried. Another was a very practical concern: the cardboard tags tied to my clothing, and to my ever-present gas mask, showing name and destination, could get wet. The ink would then run, and I would be lost forever.

"Stay out of the rain," she insisted.

In England? Is she kidding??

It took a few hours to get to our destination, but not without a little unexpected excitement. We were just a few minutes outside of London when we were attacked by a stray German fighter plane. I could see it buzzing around us, guns blazing—at least until they made us all lie down on the floor. Then, I could only hear the rat-a-tat-tat of the bullets as they slammed into the roof of the train. It was exciting, and a little scary, but I'd seen and heard all this before, right on my own doorstep.

Familiarity breeds indifference.

We duly arrived at Frome Station, and our group quickly dispersed. One of the adults told me to "Wait right here. Someone will come for you."

Five minutes went by, an eternity under the circumstances. I was still waiting for the someone, when I began to wonder if perhaps there was another train station in Frome, and whether I was at the right one. After all, we had lots of stations in London. Both above ground and below. But that, of course, was London. Not Frome.

Two minutes more, and a pretty young woman came running onto the platform. Wearing a shy smile, she came up to me and gave me a big hug.

"I'm Nellie," she said breathlessly. Since we'd never met before, I wondered how she knew that I was the boy she was supposed to meet. Being the only one on the platform must have narrowed her choices.

Taking my hand, she said, "Come on. We'll just be in time for tea." Nellie radiated warmth. Her short, straight, blond hair seemed to highlight her innocent simplicity. It was easy to like her. And anyway, even then I always had a thing for blondes. I still remembered Thelma Hodges from my Guildford days. Since Nellie proved to be the only female in my Frome life, it was also easy to develop a crush on her. So I did. Within hours.

We set off for Water Lane at the south end of town. Number 3 was one of the tiniest houses on that narrow, winding, cobblestoned street. While I was used to London's narrow, winding cobblestoned streets, this one was different: it went downhill. But as Nellie pointed out, "It goes uphill the other way." I remember thinking this was a joke, until I later realized it wasn't. Nellie was a very sweet person, but apparently not a member of the Frome intelligentsia.

Once again, I was learning that life outside flat London included things like hills, trees, and farms. It also included people walking around without gas masks. It was a relief to get rid of mine as soon as we arrived at the house. And the absence of air raids was a welcome relief.

Nellie worked as a babysitter and house cleaner. She lived alone with her cat, Puddles. I quickly understood the origin of the name. She could also have called it Piddles.

Nellie's new husband, Jack, had recently enlisted in the Royal Air Force, and was stationed somewhere in Europe.

He'd only been gone a few weeks, and since she was quite lonely, she volunteered to take in an evacuee. Me. The arrangement seemed to work well. For both of us. I missed home, but quickly shrugged off any homesickness. The house? Well, it was no Rookwood, my first evacuation experience. It was quite tiny, in fact. Minuscule, really. And cold and a little damp. The only source of heat was a small coal fire in the kitchen. Much the same as we had at home, really. And that certainly didn't help my chronic chilblain problem.

Chilblains? I hear you ask. *What the hell are they*?

Many years later, after moving to the US, I had reason to see my first American physician. I mentioned my history of chilblains. He was fascinated. He knew of them but had never seen them.

Chilblains are the result of painful inflammation of small blood vessels that occur in response to repeated exposure to cold and humid air. They're characterized by itching, red patches, swelling, and blistering on fingers and, for me, on toes. Keeping the extremities warm in cold weather helped. Central heating was the ultimate preventative treatment. But who in the poor parts of London had that? That was as rare as two consecutive, warm, sunny days. One consecutive day, maybe. But two? You're pushing your luck. Meanwhile, keep scratching the itch.

And so to school. One of the reasons why I was in Frome. Founded in 1536, Coopers' was an all-boys school, with a rich history and a highly credentialed male staff. The teachers all wore flowing black gowns, and the boys had to observe a strict school uniform code, even with wartime rationing and shortages. Structure and discipline, and need I say, an upgrade in the style and level of punishment. Most of the teachers had obviously read, and admired, Dickens. Maybe they were James Bond/007 wannabes: no license to kill, but licensed to inflict pain. Lots of pain. We were sure that at least five of them were Nazis in academic clothing: moles ready to rise up on command. One of them, Wally Treisman, spoke fluent German, for Chrissake! And masquerading as a German language teacher was, of course, the perfect cover for him.

An early surprise for me was that I had to take Latin; it was compulsory. Could have been useful if we were likely to be invaded by the armies of Julius Caesar. I can only guess how Latin must have sounded with a heavy cockney accent. I can guess—I just don't want to.

In the first week or so, I learned that these teachers were even less tolerant of talking in class than good old, ear-boxing Mr. Pickles.

"Come here, boy," Mr. Britten, our French teacher demanded. I joined him at the front of the class. "When I say, 'no talking,' I mean 'NO talking!'"

I looked up to see a tight-lipped, scowling face that knew not of warm and fuzzy. An unfriendly man who took every opportunity to reinforce his obvious contempt for little boys.

"Wait here," he snarled, and off he went.

Now I'd been around the punishment circuit many times, and knew enough to expect the cane. I quickly began to blow warm air onto my hands and rub them together to soften them for the blows to come. A wet tongue over the palms would absorb the sting. I'd been around. I could handle this.

When Gus Britten returned with a long, thin, flexible cane, the punishment book, and English teacher, Mr. Nichols, as witness, I was ready. Well, maybe not.

"Bend over!" he snapped.

Standard beatings were typically "Three" or "Six of the Best." He lashed into my tender, unprepared buttocks three times with a fury that cried out for psychoanalysis. His. Most of us on the receiving end of the action would also cry out. The bamboo cane was finally banned in 1989. A little late for me: I'd have been fifty-seven years old.

One master, who shall remain nameless, was a steady number one at the top of the bastard list. That was mathematics teacher, Mr. Drake. "Quacker" to us. Not much more than five feet tall, he always seemed to be ready for a fight. Unfortunately, only he was both armed and authorized to cause bodily harm.

He swept into class one day, gown swirling menacingly around him. He sniffed, like a wild, hungry animal sensing fresh meat. And I guess, to him, we were. Quite casually, he asked, "Who hasn't had the cane yet?" Silence. "C'mon. Who hasn't had the cane yet?" he repeated more urgently. Three hands slowly went up. Half up, actually. For a moment I thought he too would raise his hand, and say, "Heil Hitler." But no. Not yet, anyway. What followed was nine of the best, divided equally among three reluctant recipients. Easy to see why the Quacker taught maths (Britspeak for math).

Nellie and I were having afternoon tea together: fresh bread, lots of jam, cake, and a pot of strong English tea. It was always a welcome treat, especially since she served my favorite brown bread, Hovis. Even though rationing was ever-present, it seemed to be less of a hardship in the country. Locally grown fruit and vegetables were quite plentiful.

Nellie suddenly blurted out, "I'm pregnant!"

I immediately dropped my slice of bread that was bulging with blackcurrant jam. Jam-side down, of course. Knowing what the word meant, I felt myself blush. Really blush. I didn't know what to say, but I did know what to think: *It's not mine! I wasn't even 'ere.*

"Oh?" I said, hesitantly, wondering if I should say what I was thinking?

"And here's my problem," she continued. "I want to write to Jack and tell him, but I can't spell 'pregnant.' Do you know how to?"

I remained flushed, and heard myself mumbling something about having heard the word said, but never having seen it written. Which, in fact, was true. "But I fink I can guess 'ow it's spelled," I offered.

"Oh, please try," she said enthusiastically.

So I did, hesitatingly: "P-R-E-G-N-E-N-T."

She wrote it down. It looked all right to me. But, I thought, if it was wrong, well, Jack would figure it out. Then again, since Nellie told me that Jack was as uneducated as she was, and couldn't spell at all, who knows?

We had one piece of legitimate, war-related excitement. Apparently, a German plane, way off course, crashed somewhere in the area. An airman was seen to bail out. The local constable was going around the streets alerting people to watch out for him. He knocked on Number 3, talked to Nellie, and then to me, saying, "Okay, son. Keep your eyes open."

"I always do," was my smart-arsed reply. "Uverwise I keep walkin' into fings." You can see why Londoners weren't the preferred species.

I lived in Frome for a couple of months. During that time, London was again in the middle of a sustained air raid-free period. So my parents arranged for Nellie to send me back home. The train ride back took best part of a day. FedEx would have had me there in a couple of hours. Amazon could have droned me back in minutes.

I never saw or heard of Nellie again. I often wondered if Jack returned home safely, and whether their child was a boy or girl. Nellie desperately wanted a boy; perhaps that's why she "adopted" me for a while. I hope I didn't make her change her thinking.

I made a good friend in Frome, outside of school. He was a local boy, about my age, named Oliver Slade. I sometimes had trouble understanding Oliver. I told him about the warning we'd received about the "Zummerzet" dialect. He thought that was funny because his teacher had warned him about the cockney accent. I had to explain to him that he was the one with the accent. I didn't have any.

Or, as I would've said at the time: "No, mate, I ain't got no bloody accent. You 'ave."

Nellie and the Nazis
PostScript

It was easy to adjust to Somerset's clean air and colorful countryside. The green hills, blossoming trees, and abundant flowers quickly became part of my everyday surroundings.

It was hardly surprising, therefore, that when I returned to war-ravaged London, the contrast with the Somerset that I'd left behind was striking: after four long years of war, vast areas of the city lay in ruins. There were no green hills or flowers. The houses and buildings of east London were old, tired, and worn even before the war, while the structures that hadn't survived were reduced to an amorphous mix of gray-brown rubble.

But there were two colors unique to London that we could always count on: the red, double-decker bus, and the sulfurous, yellowish-green, soot-flecked, life-shortening smog we called a pea-souper. That's the London I remember so well. And nostalgically miss.

A few years after I'd left Frome, I had a homework assignment and came across the word "pregnant." I immediately thought of Nellie, and felt guilty for having misspelled it. (No, me ol' muckers. "Misspelled" ain't misspelt. It is misspelled.) And "muckers?" Ye olde cockneye worde for mates, mate.

And what of post-Coopers Frome? How did the town commemorate the wartime presence of such an illustrious scholastic institution?

Did they commission a controversial piece of sculpture? Locate an elegant plaque? Establish academic scholarships or a stimulating lecture series? Nah! Not visionary Frome. With great pride, and to celebrate the sixty-fourth year after the end of the Second World War, the town of Frome, in the county of Somerset, introduced…The Frome Cobble Wobble. A bicycle race up the cobbled streets of St. Catherine's Hill.

We clearly made a lasting impression on the Frome arts and educational communities.

17

V-1. Twelve Seconds
PreScript

"Silence is the ultimate weapon of power."

Charles de Gaulle
General & President of France

And the pregnant silence of the V-1's descent was, for me, the most frightening experience of the whole war.

V-1. Twelve Seconds
Script

Until the US entered the war, the defeat of England looked to be possible, even probable. The relentless bombing of London by the German Luftwaffe, coupled with the naval blockade of the British Isles, was intended to bring the country to its knees. And surely the enemy came close. But the Brits stiffened, resisted, and frustrated Nazi Germany. Like a desperate, out-punched boxer clinging to the ropes, London refused to go down.

When this strategy faltered, the Brits believed that Germany would invade the UK. Indeed, *Unternehmen Seelöwe* was Nazi Germany's code name for the well-planned invasion, that we came to know as "Operation Sea Lion." It was a common topic of conversation, and many believed it to be inevitable. Just in case, Tony, Mikey, and I were ready: we had a good supply of stones hidden away. And we sure as hell knew how to throw them.

But for a variety of reasons, the invasion didn't happen. And so the Battle of Britain took another turn. The heavy Allied bombing of German cities, followed by the invasion of Normandy, prompted Germany to accelerate the development of its new secret weapons—especially for use against the UK. With his new weaponry, Hitler still believed he could win the war.

Unaware, and certainly unprepared for any new form of aerial attack, calm had returned to the streets of London. The relief was everywhere. People were sure that the rest of the war would be "over there" and not "over here." After many years, too many years, the switch from "*defence to offence*" was a reason to celebrate. Well, that's what *we* thought.

When General Patton said, time to go get the bastards, he was surely thinking, "*defense to offense.*"

Had Germany given up all ideas of destroying Britain? Or did it have one final fling left? The Allied invasion of France had started, but still no fling. No sign of the Luftwaffe's return to London. And that was just fine with us. Then, dramatically, peace was shattered: the first of four V-1s were on their way to war-weary London. It was June 13, 1944, and a new era of aerial warfare had begun.

The Germans had introduced the first of their "weapons of retaliation." They called them *Vergeltungswaffen*. And this was *Vergeltungswaffe 1*. The V-1. Londoners called them flying bombs, buzz bombs, doodlebugs, anything to avoid saying *Vergeltungswaffen*. That would be too bloody difficult. And so...unEnglish.

However reluctantly, we have to give credit to the ingenuity of the German engineers. In many ways, the monsters they created were ahead of their time. The V-1 was basically a cruise missile. The first of its kind. Launched from German-occupied France at a speed of 400 mph, it took about 15 minutes to reach the heart of London, a distance of about 95 miles. It carried a 1-ton warhead.

For the next 2-3 months, the Brits were, once again, going to be preoccupied with the immediacy of survival. Nearly 10,000 V-1s were launched towards the UK. More than 2,500 reached the British capital, and at their peak, more than 100 doodlebugs were striking the UK every day. Again, Hitler expected his new weapons to crush the Londoners' spirit and bring the country to its knees. But again Londoners denied him.

Winston Churchill put it well, as he usually did: "Little does [Hitler] know the spirit of the British nation, or the tough fibre of the Londoners."

I'm not sure that we knew at the time.

Initially, the V-1s proved to be too fast for antiaircraft gunfire to be effective. Over time, however, the British defense systems learned how to manage their resources, and 2,000 V-1s were destroyed by antiaircraft fire, 2,000 by British fighter planes, and 300 by barrage balloons. The price was high: more than 6,000 Brits were killed and nearly 20,000 were injured.

So where was I during this phase of the war? I was in London, right in the middle of it, watching it unfold. On that first day, 10 V-1s were launched; four reached England. The first fell harmlessly in the county of Kent, southeast of London. The second landed in Bethnal Green, a mile or so from where I lived. I was close enough to see that historic event. A solitary plane was a strange enough sight. But this one was even more unusual: flames spewed from its cylindrical tail as it streaked across the sky. My first thought was that it was an airplane that had been hit, and would soon be spiraling its way down to earth. I'd seen that so many times before. But not this time. It kept going straight ahead until its engine stalled and stopped. It then fell silently until, on contact with land, it ended its journey in a huge fireball. The explosion seemed to rumble on forever.

I couldn't wait to get to school to tell my friends what I'd seen. Unfortunately, they didn't exactly embrace my description of a plane that looked like a glowing cigar with wings. I lost a lot of credibility that day.

Seeing this sequence of events from a safe distance, I was left with the thought that this was just another wartime threat to adjust to and accept. In the daylight, it wasn't so bad: we could see where it was headed. It was also bloody exciting. And its newness added even more fascination.

But at night, in the dark, when that raspy engine that sounded as if it needed an oil change, sputtered and died, we had no idea where it might land. It was like playing Russian roulette, repeatedly, night after night.

As the V-1s droned overhead, I willed them to keep flying. To keep moving until the sound of their engines began to recede. But if a V-1 was overhead when its engine cut out, we had about twelve seconds to know whether the next explosion was to be the last thing we'd ever hear. That period of silence became increasingly terrifying. Heart-poundingly terrifying. The sound of bombs as they whistled down to earth was scary enough, but the silence of a descending V-1, for me, became the most frightening experience of the war. After nearly five years of conflict, at the age of eleven, I was now old enough to understand, and old enough to have learned fear. The fear that filled those oppressive twelve seconds.

I'd sometimes silently count the seconds until the explosion. Or, I'd scrunch my face up as hard as I could until I heard the boom. Other times I'd hold my breath. I wasn't the praying kind, so that wasn't an option. I came close on occasion, but I couldn't look up to the heavens for comfort: death was up there. My mother would often take my hand and silently squeeze it tight. Sometimes so tight that it would hurt. Other times, she'd hug me to her, trying to protect me from whatever was to come. It never became easier to survive the horror of those silences, and that awful feeling of helplessness. We simply had to wait for the seconds to pass. Those agonizingly slow twelve seconds. To wait for the explosion. To wait for death.

One...two...three...four...five...six...seven...eight...nine...ten...eleven.........

V-1. Twelve Seconds
PostScript

Winston Churchill had the courage and the commitment to make a number of unusually difficult wartime decisions. Several, costing many civilian lives, were disclosed well after the war.

The first is well documented. It took place in November, 1940. By intercepting German radio messages encrypted with the Enigma machine, the British government had advance warning of a major attack on the city of Coventry in England. "The Coventry Blitz." In what was obviously a painful decision, Winston Churchill ordered that no defensive measures should be taken to protect Coventry, to avoid alerting the Germans that their secret code had been broken. Many hundreds of Coventry citizens died in that attack.

A second occasion when innocent British civilians were sacrificed is less well reported. It occurred in June, 1944.

England was again under aerial attack. This time, by V-1s. Churchill had, once again, made a Coventry-like decision, benefiting London inhabitants at the cost of those in Kent.

In their reports to Germany, a group of double agents were instructed by the British to exaggerate the number of V-1s dropping to the north and west of London, and minimize the numbers hitting central London and the south. This convinced the German engineers that the missiles were overshooting their targets, and persuaded them to shorten the flight times. The result was that nearly 1500 V-1s fell on less populated areas in Kent.

This subterfuge was kept secret, not only to deceive the Germans, but also to keep the civilian population of the southeast suburbs from knowing that their lives were being endangered to make central London safer.

So thank you, Mr. Prime Minister. You might just have kept me alive a little longer. But I hate to think that some poor sod in Kent might have died in my stead.

Much later, Churchill expressed the belief, that his Coventry decision shortened his life by 20 years. Throw in another 20 for Kent, and he apparently gave up 40 years. Since he died at the age of 90, left in peace, he'd have lived to 130. Unless he ran out of cigars and whisky.

Which leads me to comment on his personal indulgences. Being born into the privileges of the upper classes, as Churchill was, had its advantages. While the great man grossly mismanaged his personal finances, being "easily satisfied with the best," the assumption of his wealth apparently supported his ability to routinely live beyond his means. Wealthy benefactors helped as, eventually, did his extraordinary and salable talent with words.

But all's forgiven, Winnie, we're just glad you were there for us.

18

V-2. Flying Gas Pipes
PreScript

And the rockets' red glare,
the bombs bursting in air…

"The Star-Spangled Banner"
American National Anthem
Words by Francis Scott Key

These words always remind me of the
London Blitz: Lots of rockets;
lots of bombs. Too many of both.

V-2. Flying Gas Pipes
Script

It started with a bang. A really big bang. An explosion that many said was louder than any that we'd experienced during the earlier bombing raids over London. Or the ongoing V-1 attacks. In other words, it was bloody loud!

It was a gentle September evening in 1944 when, just a few miles away, the first Big Bang boomed. Initially, there was nothing. Then, the explosion. No one saw or heard anything unusual, until it happened. Other "mysterious" explosions followed and, instinctively perhaps, we all knew that this was the beginning of a new Nazi nightmare.

It seemed strange, that for leadership that never tried to understate the horrors of the war we were fighting, the British government would conceal the cause of these new explosions, blaming them on defective gas mains. Gas mains? Really! Was this to guard against panic? If so, they should have known that Londoners could handle the truth. Stiff upper lips were everywhere. We all had 'em. Had to. Nevertheless, it was many weeks before Churchill, downplaying the relevance of the V-2s, revealed that England had been under rocket attack by a new German weapon.

Ironically, many were aware of the nature of the attack within hours of the first explosion. With typical good humor, and a touch of sarcasm, Londoners referred to these new weapons as "Flying Gas Pipes." And anyway, pieces of rocket tail fins found near the newly-formed craters weren't exactly compatible with exploding gas pipes.

Just as the V-1 campaign was tapering off, the more advanced and far deadlier V-2s begin to rain. And reign. And this time, we had no effective umbrella. No defense. This was Hitler's desperate attempt to claim victory. A last throw of the dice. But last throw or not, he did strike a powerful blow, and got a big bang for his buck. Well, for his Deutschmark, anyway. And regardless of the currency, his bang was certainly big!

The V-2 missiles were quite revolutionary. They reached speeds of nearly 4,000 mph, had a range of 200 miles, and packed a one-ton warhead. Plunging to Earth at nearly 2,000 mph, and faster than sound, they hit the ground before they were ever heard. And very few people witnessed them in flight.

While, over time, we learned how to defend ourselves against the V-1s, our normal defenses were useless against this new weapon. There was no defense. We could only wait to see where the next rocket would land. Meanwhile, about 1,500 V-2s were directed at London over a 6-7 month period. Nearly 3,000 civilians were killed, and another 6,500 injured. The world's first modern ballistic missile, the first man-made object to reach the edge of space, was a terrifying experience.

Even in the middle of all this horror, there was a lighter moment. There always is. Soon after the defective gas main explanation was largely debunked, and the V-2s were recognized for what they were, Teddy Jackson, one of my school pals, returned to school after a few days' absence. He announced, with great pride, that his house had been "nearly destroyed" by a V-2. We were impressed. As the facts unfolded, however, we learned that his house had suffered only minor damage. Teddy explained that away by claiming that they were hit by a small V-2. Not so. The origin of his explosion actually proved to be a defective gas main. No fragments of rocket tail fins were ever found, but pieces of gas pipe were everywhere. The government strategists who first came up with the gas pipe explanation were delighted. Teddy was very disappointed.

There was, of course, no small V-2; they were all big, bad, and deadly!

The very first V-2 fell a few miles from my house, and one of the last was within a mile. I heard that one. Couldn't help it. And in between, it was another game of Russian roulette. How long could we continue to beat the odds? At frequent intervals, day or night, enormous explosions shattered London life. There was no warning, just the double-crack of the supersonic rocket.

We did have one approach to defend against the V-2s: misdirection. Just as our double agents exploited that idea defending against the V-1s, so they also leaked information that the V-2s were overshooting their London targets. To a degree, it worked. For a while, the V-2s began to fall short of their objectives, as the Germans "corrected" their settings—and bombed the hell out of Kent. Again.

I still find it surprising to accept that many people feared the V-2 rockets far more than the V-1 doodlebugs. Even now, I can feel the feelings. Yes, an enormous explosion with absolutely no warning was an immediate and violent shock. But it was quick. Emphatic. Final. Surely a V-1, and the slow and painful wait for possible death that it inflicted, was worse. Those twelve hellish seconds of terrifying silence still haunt me.

But in the grand scheme of things, did it make any difference to the thousands of Londoners who gave up their lives to German aerial attacks, whether it was an "ordinary" bomb, a V-1, or a V-2 that was the instrument of death? Dead was dead. More than 40,000 innocent people were killed. They weren't soldiers or military personnel. They were civilians: mostly the old, the disabled, women, and children. Yet the Germans dismissed this when they subsequently objected to the retaliatory Allied bombing of cities like Dresden.

No sympathy from me. No other cheek-turning. No eye for an eye. I wanted two eyes for an eye. Maybe three.

V-2. Flying Gas Pipes
PostScript

The Big Bang Theory is the generally accepted explanation for the origin of the universe. At its simplest, it all began about 13.7 billion years ago from a single point of dense matter. In essence, life began with a Big Bang. When the V-2s arrived, life for thousands of Londoners ended in a Big Bang. Devastating. But tidy?

In addition to a "Bomb Sight Project" pinpointing the locations of the thousands of German bombs that fell on London, a second effort, still ongoing some seventy years later, is designed to map all the V-2 strikes on London interactively. Its current status can be seen on the internet:

https://londonist.com/2013/06/v2

Together, they bring the massive aerial attacks on London during World War II into sharp focus. Examining these extraordinary records dramatically demonstrates that British

Street, and my house on it, was right there in the middle of all the action. Yet we survived largely unscathed. Looks to be impossible.

The card-carrying Nazi Wernher von Braun directed Germany's V-2 program. After the war, the conscience-less bastard was co-opted to lead America's space program, building the Saturn rocket that carried Apollo 11 to the moon. I have difficulty with the morality of the American opportunism. I understand it. I just don't like it.

For any student of World War II history, the Holocaust was one of the most inhuman, barbaric crimes perpetrated by Nazi Germany. The wealth of evidence supporting the existence of the Holocaust is overwhelming. I didn't have to be there to believe it happened. Consequently, I've never taken those who claim it was all a hoax too seriously. I dismiss such assertions as absurd.

I now find myself immersed in a different claim of a hoax. This time I was directly involved. This time, my reaction is not a dismissal of the naysayers, but outrage.

In recent times, now more than seventy years later, there have been many expressions of disbelief that the V-1s and V-2s ever existed. "It was all a hoax," the disbelievers claim.

Their arguments cover a broad spectrum of issues. They doubt that the Nazis could have had such sophisticated auto-piloting and rocket technology back in the '40s. They believe that the V-1s were actually piloted by volunteers who were prepared to meet their deaths in the fashion of the Japanese kamikaze pilots; that the V-1 killing of thousands of civilians was highly improbable; that in general, the V-1s and V-2s simply didn't look credible; that it's extremely suspicious that while poor sections of east London were destroyed, Buckingham Palace and the Houses of Parliament were not (frankly, I'd always wondered about that); and finally, that the British government faked the existence of the V-weapons to keep the people "frightened." To the contrary, of course, there is much evidence to support the fact that the government downplayed the effectiveness of the V-1s and V-2s, hoping to persuade the Germans that their V-attacks weren't worth continuing.

Yes, I'm sure there were instances of inaccurate reporting. Many instances. Inevitable under the circumstances. But that doesn't justify total disbelief of what were well-recorded events of that period.

From my point of view, as an eleven-year-old boy being slap-bang in the middle of the Blitz, I wasn't relying on government reports to tell me that the V-weapons were real. I saw. I heard. I counted dead bodies. Unless it's suggested that nearly ten million Londoners were hypnotized, no one could fake the twelve seconds of hell that the V-1s put us through.

That was no fake. That was no hoax.

19

V-3. The Shell Game
PreScript

"The trouble with Germans is not that they fire shells,
but that they engrave them with quotations from Kant."

Karl Kraus
Austrian satirist

Immanuel Kant
German philosopher

V-3. The Shell Game
Script

After surviving the first two *Vergeltungswaffen*—the V-1 doodlebugs, and the V-2 Big Bangers—there was much speculation about what a V-3 might be. I was sure it would be some kind of invisible ray gun. Well, I was just a kid.

In this regard, I'm reminded of Albert Einstein's prophetic comment: "I know not with what weapons World War III will be fought, but World War IV will be fought with sticks and stones." At the time, it might have been said that whatever the V-3 and the Allied response proved to be, the V-4 might well be sticks and stones. But speculation apart, there was indeed a V-3. Glad to say it didn't impact our side of the Channel. Not sure we'd have been able to survive yet another secret weapon.

Nevertheless, experience had taught us to prepare for the next wave of terror. No one doubted German ingenuity to create weapons of death and destruction, or for the Nazis' willingness to use them. London's rapidly filling cemeteries were a testament to that.

And so we waited for secret weapon V-3. Whatever it was to be. And perhaps V-4 after that?

Which prompts me to raise a question, one that, at the time, bothered me and my ready-to-fight mates. How come the German bastards had all the Vs: the V-1, V-2, and all the other V's yet to appear? Where were the Allied weapons specialists? What were we doing? Yes, I know the Americans were busy developing the atomic bomb, and the Brits were breaking the Enigma code and developing radar. But where were all the nomenclature specialists? Couldn't we have had, say, an X-series of weapons? Or perhaps a Z-series? Apparently not. For whatever reason. But in a way, we went one better. We forced the Nazis into aborting its V-series by a sneaky maneuver: we claimed the V-4 for ourselves.

We had it. And they didn't!

And even as a young boy, I personally participated in implementing its punishing power. I'll tell you more about that shortly.

V-3. The Shell Game
PostScript

It wasn't until well after the war that I became aware of what the V-3 actually was. Referred to as a V-3 cannon, my initial thought was that it must be a new printer. A real breakthrough. One that uses a lot less ink.

Not so. It was, in fact, a cannon and not a Canon. This was no old-fashioned gun: it was a gigantic "supergun." Some 430 feet long. I'd have called it a whopper back then. It could fire 310 lb especially propelled shells. The Germans called it *Fleißiges Lieschen*, Busy Lizzie. Projected to fire 300 shells per hour, it was well named. This cannon was intended to blast the hell out of London. Or should that be blast the hell *into* London? Fortunately, Allied bombing raids successfully rendered the superguns useless. Thanks, chaps. I owe you one. Actually, I owe you many.

The original Nazi plan was to have twenty-five of these monsters trained on London. Being on the receiving end of 7,500 shells per hour, I don't think too much of our fair city would have survived.

So there you are. Or more to the point, here I are. Thanks to the US and UK air forces, I live…if not to fight another day, at least to live one.

20

V-4. Victory
PreScript

"Quitters never win, winners never quit, but those who Never win and never quit are idiots."

Anonymous

V-4. Victory
Script

So V-4 was ours! *Our* secret weapon. V-4-Victory. V-for-Victory. Great move. Whether the Germans had plans for a V-4 weapon or not, we don't know. But we do know that the Brits swept in and grabbed Number 4. We might not have been prepared for war with guns and planes, but we were ready to fight with words. And no one was better at that than our fearless leader, Winston Churchill.

Churchill popularized the phrase V-for-Victory, and the two-fingered V-for-Victory hand gesture. The V-campaign was heavily publicized by the BBC, and soon became highly popular throughout Europe. It used no imported materials, it produced no waste products, and was cost-effective. At the time, it was wildly rumored that excessive use of the gesture could lead to severe osteoarthritic metacarpals, complicated by Dupuytren Contracture. But that proved to be little more than a Nazi propaganda counterattack. Just kidding about the arthritis.

With his usual stately oratory, Churchill announced: "The V sign is the symbol of the unconquerable will of the occupied territories and a portent of the fate awaiting Nazi tyranny. So long as the peoples continue to refuse all collaboration with the invader, it is sure that his cause will perish and Europe will be liberated."

Wherever he went, Churchill was sure to flourish a V-sign with his first and second fingers, promising victory. But he did have to be careful. With the palm side of his hand away from him, it was the Victory sign. With the palm side towards him, it was the equivalent of the offensive American middle finger gesture, and then some. Depending on the circumstances, this V meant either "Fuck Off," or "Fuck You." And if you really want your gesture to be emphatic, you flicked the V upwards from the wrist or elbow. It's then as insulting as it gets. I knew that. Most Londoners knew that. So did the Aussies, the New Zealanders, and the Canadians. But did Churchill? In many pictures, he's seen with his palm facing inwards instead of out. Some argued that since the "wrong" V would only be known to the working classes, his aristocratic background would leave him unaware of the other meaning of the V sign. Others say he used it to insult the enemy without them even being aware of it. Only Winnie knew for sure. He certainly had a dry sense of humor, so who knows?

As the hand gestures and the graffiti spread throughout Europe, the Nazis became increasingly irritated. In desperation, they claimed that the V stood for the German word "Viktoria," and that its use by civilians was a sign of support for a German victory. Too little; too late. The V-4 was ours. V for Victory belonged to the good guys.

Whether or not the Brits' early ownership of the V-4 was a preemptive strike or not, we'll never know. It's possible that omitting the V-4, and going directly from a V-3 weapon to a V-5, would have been far too disorderly for any German to contemplate. Maybe. Maybe not. But we do know that the V-3 was Nazi Germany's final *Vergeltungswaffe*.

V-4. Victory
PostScript

While Winston Churchill popularized the V for Victory sign, credit for its origin and broad European appeal during World War II belongs to a Belgian. The use of V as a symbol of defiant resistance to tyranny was first proposed by Victor de Laveleye, a member of the Belgian Parliament in exile in England.

In a broadcast on January 14, 1941, Laveleye suggested the V campaign, where V is the first letter of the word Victory in French, Flemish (Belgium's language), and English. It also works for a few other countries like Spain and Italy. It caught on, and the V symbol quickly began to appear as defiant graffiti in many Nazi-occupied countries. But I still wonder how the Poles, whose word for victory is zwycięstwo, the Hungarians, győzelem, the Dutch, overwinning, and others, handled the campaign.

Laveleye's first name was Victor. So could all this be just a self-styled ego trip? No way! The man played tennis for Belgium in the Olympic games of 1920 and 1924, for chrissake. That's good enough for me.

Misusing the V-sign continues to offer a potential downside to the unaware user. When George Bush Senior visited Australia, he attempted to be friendly to a group of protesters in Canberra by offering them the V (for Peace) sign. Unfortunately, his inward-facing palm didn't exactly endear him to the locals. Remember, the Aussies knew.

21

No Tears for Dresden
PreScript

Prior to World War II, Dresden was referred to as "The Florence on the Elbe." It was considered to be one of the world's most beautiful cities, its architecture and art treasures being held in particularly high esteem.

Dresden had a rich history, having been established as a German colony in 1216. The city had been attacked, restored, and rebuilt many times, but since the mid-19th century, it had remained peaceful and prosperous...

No Tears for Dresden
Script

…Peaceful and prosperous, that is, until February 13, 1945.

Over a three-day period, British and American bombers dropped nearly 4,000 tons of bombs and incendiary devices on the city of Dresden. Basically flattening the whole area. The Allies had decided that retaliation of this magnitude was necessary to shorten the war and, since an estimated 25,000 people were killed, I like to think it did.

Suddenly, Londoners were talking about Dresden—wherever the hell that was. I was twelve at the time and until the bombing raid, which we discussed in school, Dresden was a new name and place to me. But as the details of the bombing became known, there was an immediate reaction of satisfaction. We had struck back. After years of being attacked by bombs, incendiaries, V-1 flying bombs, and V-2 rockets, and losing tens of thousands of innocent lives, we'd fought back. In kind. To many of us it was revenge, pure and simple. And yes, sweet. People celebrated. Up to a point. The Brits of that day were a civilized people, and for many, the satisfaction of punishing the bully, slowly gave way to sadness. Not regret. But sadness that it was necessary.

The Allied attack was carried out just a few months before the end of the war in Europe. But how could we know, definitively, just how long hostilities might linger? The issue of whether the destruction of Dresden at that time was justified became quite contentious within the British government. Had the Brits and the Americans sunk to the level of ruthless savagery shown by Nazi Germany? Will time tell? Maybe. Maybe not.

No Tears for Dresden
PostScript

The morality of the destruction of Dresden continues to be at issue. To this day. The bombing has been used by Holocaust deniers and pro-Nazi polemicists who claim a moral equivalence between the war crimes committed by the Nazis and the killing of German civilians by Allied bombing raids. Bullshit!

On the one hand, the Nazi propagandists, and all the latter-day moralists, point to the lost beauty of Dresden, claim grossly inflated numbers of victims, insist that Dresden should not have been a military target, and cling to the fact that the attack was too close to the end of the war.

On the other hand, Germany's own Weapons Office listed 127 factories in Dresden that were supplying its army with materiel. In 1978, the US Air Force finally released a classified report stating that there were 110 factories and 50,000 workers in the city supporting the German war effort at the time of the raid. Further, the British officials described Dresden as "A mass of munitions works, an intact government centre, and a key transportation point to the east." Following the raid, they added, in quiet understatement, "It is now none of these things." I liked that. And finally, it should be noted that the Allies were committed to provide air support for the Soviet approach to Berlin, where bombing the city would prevent any counterattack centered in Dresden.

In all this debate, one of the most disappointing chapters in the glorious wartime leadership of British Prime Minister Winston Churchill was the Dresden bombing. Known for his hawkishly aggressive positions on confronting the barbarism of Nazi Germany, and clearly the final arbiter of the bombing, he later tried to distance himself from it. Disappointingly, Churchill refused to fully acknowledge the contributions and sacrifices made by the RAF Bomber Command during the Dresden raids.

Why, Winnie, why? It's said that you were concerned about adverse comment in the US press. Maybe. Or were you already positioning yourself for a postwar Nobel Peace Prize? With your "unpeaceful" wartime record, I'm surprised you were even nominated for it. Settle for the Nobel Prize for Literature that you did deserve, and duly received.

Regardless of the morality issue, let's keep in mind the telling words of Sir Arthur Harris, Head of the RAF Bomber Command: "The Nazis entered this war under the rather childish delusion that they were going to bomb everyone else, and nobody was going to bomb them. At Rotterdam, London, Warsaw and half a hundred other places, they put their rather naive theory into operation. They sowed the wind, and now they are going to reap the whirlwind."

Amen to that.

For some, the feeling of justifiable retaliation may fade with time. For some, but not for me. With the cold objectivity created by the lapse of some seventy years, and my own advanced age, the view I have now is precisely the same view I had as a twelve-year-old: the destruction of Dresden was fully justified. No regrets. Save one: that too many young and courageous British and American flyers were lost during the Dresden raids.

Unavoidably, memories of the horrors of the London Blitz ran deep in 1945, as they still do for the survivors. To my mind, there was no moral equivalence between the loss of life in London and in Dresden, regardless of the numbers of lives lost on each side. It may not impress the historian, but the differences were surely significant to the Londoners of those Blitz years. Brits were murdered over an extended period of time. Many years. It was akin to being tortured, day after day, night after night, indefinitely it seemed. Waiting for death. It wasn't a question of if, but when. The Dresden citizens, on the other hand, suffered their losses over a period of hours. Unquestionably brutal, of course, but given the objectives of the mission, it was relatively humane—if the annihilation of so many civilians can ever be humane.

Under the circumstances, the best I can now do is to take the moral low ground.

Some fifty years after the war, and following the reunification of Germany, I paid my first visit to Dresden. A number of visible wartime scars remained. Mindful of the ultimate price paid by so many Londoners during the Blitz, I still felt no regret for the Allied bombing. I did feel anger, however.

During my visit, I learned that a British charity, the Dresden Trust, had been formed in 1993 to solicit funds for the rebuilding of the city. The Trust had raised nearly a million dollars from 2,000 people and 100 companies in Britain. That angered me. It suggested guilt, and there should have been none.

Surely that money could have been better spent on the children of the RAF flyers who were killed in the raids.

In 2004, Queen Elizabeth II hosted a concert in Berlin to raise money for the reconstruction of the *Frauenkirche*, Dresden's Lutheran church. The visit was accompanied by speculation in the British and German press, over a possible apology for the attacks. I'm glad to say that none was offered. Equally, and appropriately, the US has never apologized for the atomic bomb destruction of Hiroshima and Nagasaki in Japan. Nor should they ever.

22

And Peace
PreScript

"The time of universal peace is near
Prove this a prosp'rous day,
The three-nooked world
Shall bear the olive freely."

William Shakespeare
Anthony and Cleopatra
Act 4; Scene 6

Ah, but for how long?

And Peace
Script

The end of World War II seemed to come abruptly. One moment we were still at war, and the next, it was over. Everyone seemed to be smiling. The sound of easy laughter, rare for so long, was in the air. Words and phrases like "Finally," "Peace," "We Won!" were on everyone's lips. Relief was palpable. Sighs of emotional exhaustion, perhaps. But we had survived.

A week after Adolf Hitler's dramatic suicide, the Allies accepted Germany's unconditional surrender. It was May 8, 1945. A few days shy of six long and painful years after it all began on September 3, 1939. This was Victory in Europe; VE Day. Japan held out for another few months, until atomic bombs dropped on Hiroshima and Nagasaki hastened their acceptance of reality. Victory over Japan, VJ Day, followed on August 15, 1945.

I used to believe in negotiation as a way to peace. Sometimes. Maybe. Not always. And certainly not with World War II-era Nazi Germany and Japan. Peace with them had to be through victory. Crushing victory. The destruction of Dresden was necessary. Hiroshima and Nagasaki too. That was a language they understood. The only language. I learned that as a wartime kid.

To celebrate VE Day, street parties were held all over Britain. I well remember ours. A series of tables, set end to end, the whole length of the street, were filled with dozens of us kids. Excited as all hell. Many were friends of mine; others I'd never seen before. It didn't matter. We were all survivors. There were flowers, paper hats, and more food and drink than I'd seen in years. I couldn't help wondering where it all came from. Everyone seemed to be having a good time, and kept saying something celebratory, as if it might evaporate if we stopped saying it. No more gas masks, blackouts, taking shelter, and scanning the skies for signs of the enemy and for new forms of death. From all the food that suddenly appeared, I was quite certain that rationing must also be over. I'm sure I drooled over the thought of limitless chocolate now to come—as if my mother would even have allowed such a thing, even in times of plenty. But I was a little ahead of myself—or at least ahead of the authorities. Way ahead of them, in fact.

The war ended in 1945, and yet UK rationing continued for nine more years.

Nine more bloody years.

Until July, 1954. I didn't understand that at the time. The reason for the delay was simple enough—money. But I said all this earlier. So why am I saying it again? Because a kid deprived is a kid depraved.

The end of the war in Europe coincided with the beginning of my teenage years. It was May, 1945. A time to be free again. No more air raids to keep me close to home. I had room to move around. Sort of. We still had, and would continue to have for many years, some unusual restrictions on our movements. We were now in and surrounded by extensive areas of bomb damage, the crumbling remains of unstable houses and buildings, and the cordoned-off sections of other potential danger.

One of the most hazardous environmental problems we frequently encountered was the presence of unexploded bombs: they were routinely discovered and removed, sometimes with disastrous consequences. A sudden, violent explosion was a dramatic reminder of this new phase of postwar life.

The absence of new threats happily left us with more personal freedom and flexibility. Suddenly I could come home after dark and not have to endure parental lectures. It was a freedom that had been absent for far too long. It was only after it was given back that I realized it had been taken away. It was a small hardship in the grand scheme of things, but a meaningful one in the life of a teenager eager to explore the world around him. Well, I was nearly a teenager.

It was now a time to adjust to life without a constant threat of death. In many ways, and for so long, I knew little else. A return to peace, and an opportunity to resume normal everyday living, was initially a welcome relief. In other ways, after years of unending excitement and danger, it was somewhat anticlimactic. In some bizarre way, I missed those turbulent times.

It seemed to me that adults would continue saying things like "We're still alive," forever. But then they'd suddenly stop and, as if driven by guilt, would remember family, neighbors, and friends who were no longer with us. Those who paid the ultimate price for our survival. While my own family was lucky to survive largely intact, other families I knew didn't. I had several friends, both from the neighborhood and from school, whose fathers never returned from battle. A few teachers and friendly shopkeepers would not be returning either.

And Peace
PostScript

"This is your victory! It is the victory of the cause of freedom…This is your hour…It's a victory of the great British nation…We stood, alone…The lights went out and the bombs came down. But every man, woman, and child in the country had no thought of quitting the struggle. London can take it. So we came back after long months from the jaws of death, out of the mouth of hell…We have emerged from (our) deadly struggle."

Winston Churchill, British Prime Minister
Addressing the British People
Victory-in-Europe Day, May 8, 1945

During World War II, Clement Attlee was the leader of the Labour Party and Deputy Prime Minister in Churchill's coalition government. Just two weeks after Victory in Europe was declared, the UK held a national election. Astonishingly, the immensely popular but conservative wartime leader Sir Winston Churchill was defeated by Attlee's Labour Party in a landslide.

Churchill, who was known for his many witty but biting remarks, described Attlee as "A modest man, who has much to be modest about." Nevertheless, people looked at Winnie as a wartime leader, and his job was done. I was sad to see him go. My mother was quite distraught.

I was fascinated to learn that, even now, more than seventy years after the war, unexploded bombs continue to be unearthed. Literally. In 2008, one of them, a 2,000-pound bomb was found in Bow, where I had lived during the Blitz. It was still ticking when the bomb disposal experts removed it. From 2006-2009, more than 15,000 items of ordinance, bombs, grenades, etc., were found. About 30,000 tons—that's 60 million pounds—of high explosives were dropped on London during WWII. Not all exploded, of course, and many remain buried tens of feet below the ground. They're typically discovered during construction activities. Thus, over the years, finding an unexploded bomb in postwar London has become a way of life. And sadly, on occasion, a way of death. A helluva way to keep the British worker from leaning idly on his shovel.

The total number of deaths associated with World War II, both military and civilian, were estimated to be more than 75 million. The breakdown was as follows: Allies: UK, including British Empire countries, 580,000; US, 410,000; France, 600,000; Soviet Union, 27 million. Losses by the Axis countries: Germany, 7 million; Japan, 3 million; Italy, 500,000. Mind-boggling numbers.

To clarify, Northern Ireland is part of the United Kingdom, and is included in the UK total. Eire (or simply, Ireland) was then, and still is, an independent country; it remained neutral, and suffered very few deaths. It was a generally held view in London that Eire was more pro-Nazi than neutral. Saddens me to think about that: some of my best friends are Irish—both north and south of the border. And the Swiss? They also remained neutral and incurred fewer than 100 casualties. In their case, they were too busy making cuckoo clocks and money.

Postface

Some fifty years after the end of World War II, my new wife and I traveled to the UK to visit all of the places where I'd lived and/or attended school during the war. Surely a fun trip into nostalgia. For me, anyway.

We started with my "ancestral home" at Number 10, British Street. When I finally left it, a few years after the war, it was still standing. "Bloody, but unbowed." Two or three other houses on the street were gutted—little more than shells of their former structures. The rest had suffered varying degrees of war-related damage, but all had survived. And that's how I'd left them.

And now? This time? Not so! Number 10 was gone. As were the other houses either side of Number 10, and those across the street. All of them. In fact, the whole of British Street was gone! It had, in fact, been cannibalized by the adjacent St. Clements Hospital. So, as if repeating it makes it easier to accept, Number 10 was gone. As were all of the houses of my old friends: Donald, Tony, and Mikey. And yes, that of my first lady love, my show-me-yours-and-I'll-show-you-mine gal, Rosie, leaving me with no opportunity to check on her "fing." The street itself had been totally reconfigured, and now seemed to be little more than an afterthought of a side street parking lot. What was left? Memories. Still sharp, but untouchably relegated to the mind.

We checked on my primary school next, Malmesbury Road. Founded in 1885. Bits of the old place were still there, but not many. The structure had been substantially modified. Miss Hunt and Mr. Pickles would have been excessively ancient, so I decided not to go looking for them. I couldn't take the risk that Miss Hunt might still threaten to sit on me, and sadistic Mr. Pickles would immediately want to box my ears again; they're still ringing from the last time.

A short distance from my primary school was Coopers, my old grammar school. It was founded in 1536, give or take a few weeks, so yes, I do mean "old." I last saw Coopers' in nearby Tredegar Square. And it should still have been there. But it wasn't. Like my British Street home, it too was gone. Sometime earlier, the school had apparently moved to Upminster, some twenty miles away, becoming co-ed in the process. The teachers from my grammar school days would also have been long dead, but still available for many a nightmare appearance. How can we forget "'Quacker' Drake," the Nazi bastard?

So, the rediscovery of my London home and schools of those war years wasn't going too smoothly. In fact, it was scarcely going at all. But, what the hell, it was a rare, sunny, and warm day, even for midsummer, and it was noon. Time for a pint and a sandwich. Better yet, a "Plowman's Lunch"—a chunk of crusty bread, English cheese, apple, pickled onions and that pint I mentioned, the thought of which was beginning to induce severe salivation. The old Kings Arms pub at the top end of British Street, one of my early haunts, was beckoning. We strolled back to where it was—or at least, where it used to be. Been there since 856 BC, as best I recall. But no longer. It too was gone. It was enough to drive me to drink—if I could get one.

The journey "home" was already proving to be depressing. But we were committed, so it was on to Guilford in the county of Surrey. You may recall that I spent some time there as an evacuee, staying in that palatial mansion called Rookwood. Number 26, Portsmouth Road, set so beautifully in a vast acreage of lush countryside, remained vividly etched in my mind. Alas, that's where it must remain. And only there. We found Portsmouth Road easily enough. But the mansion and its magnificent grounds? Long gone. In its place, dozens of flats and townhouses. A whole community.

Judging from the ads we saw, this was now an upscale spread, featured as an easy, thirty-mile commute from London. Most of the new inhabitants who could afford the absurdly expensive homes were apparently heirs, Russian oil billionaires, showbiz people, and professional athletes. At least that's what one of the residents told us. He didn't tell us which one he was. Nor did we find out what was left of my wartime hosts, the Brake family. As I looked around, my mind drifted back to the sadistic, anti-London teacher who beat the hell out of me, to my first love, the beautiful Thelma Hodges, and, most vividly, to my groping, bosom buddy, Agnes. I'll especially miss the "touching" relationship Agnes and I enjoyed during the '40s, when I was young and innocent. Well, I was certainly young, and innocent too—until Agnes decided otherwise.

And lastly, it was on to Frome in Somerset. I couldn't find the temporary school we used while I was there, nor could I find anyone old enough to remember where it might have been. But I did find Number 3, Water Lane, where I stayed with dear, Preggie Nellie. With no heat or hot water, I could only imagine that her rent was just a few quid a week. That was then, of course. Those tiny dwellings are now dressed up, and described as "desirable cottages in the country." And selling for something between too much and outrageous. They may even have heat and hot water. For a few quid more, of course.

In the grand scheme of things, the places I'd lived in and the schools I'd attended weren't really that important, were they? Certainly less so than the people in my early life in England. Sadly, my wartime family, friends, and neighbors were all gone.

As I too must be.

TTFN.

About the Author

Charles Berkoff grew up as a cockney in London, England. After surviving "The Blitz," he entered the British pharmaceutical industry; he was fifteen at the time. Five years later, he opted to pursue an academic career, graduating from the University of London with a first class honors (summa cum laude) degree in chemistry. He went on to receive his PhD in organic chemistry at Imperial College, University of London, in the laboratories of Professor Sir Derek Barton, Nobel laureate. As an authentic organic chemist, he's proud to say that he's never been treated with pesticides or fertilizers.

Based on his scientific achievements, they told him he should go far; it became ugly when they insisted. And so he came to America as a Fulbright Research Fellow at the Johns Hopkins University in Baltimore, Maryland. He subsequently joined the American pharmaceutical industry, spending many years as Director, Research and Development, GlaxoSmithKline, in Philadelphia, and then as President and CEO of the biotechnology company Antigenics, Inc. In 1994, he moved to Sarasota, Florida, and founded CEBRAL, Inc., a Drug Discovery and Development Consulting Organization. He still serves as its President and CEO.

Charles enjoys duplicate bridge, cricket, competitive swimming, and tennis. As a loyal US citizen, he patiently waits to be invited to join the US Davis Cup Team. If selected, he promises to bring balls.

He's published over seventy scientific papers and patents, and another thirty or so humorous pieces in magazines and online. *PreMedicated Murder*, his first full-length novel, won two Florida Authors and Publishers awards, one for Humor and the other for Adult Fiction Mystery. That encouraged him to continue his late-life writing career. More recently, he published his collection of short stories under the title, *The Catcher Goes Awry…and Other Odds and Sods.*

Charles lives in Edenic Sarasota with his wife, Heide, their rescue dog, Landy, and his two embarrassed tennis rackets.

charlesberkoff@gmail.com
www.charlesberkoff.com
www.premedicatedmurder.com

Printed in Great Britain
by Amazon